Also by Arnold B. Kanter
from Catbird Press

The Handbook of Law Firm Mismanagement
Advanced Law Firm Mismanagement
The Ins & Outs of Law Firm Mismanagement

Was That a *Tax* Lawyer Who Just Flew Over?

From Outside the Offices of
Fairweather, Winters & Sommers

by
ARNOLD B. KANTER

Illustrated by Paul Hoffman

CATBIRD PRESS

Text © 1996 Arnold B. Kanter
Illustrations © Paul Hoffman
All rights reserved.

No part of this book may be used or reproduced in any manner without written permission, except in the context of reviews.

CATBIRD PRESS, 16 Windsor Road, North Haven, CT 06473
800-360-2391, catbird@pipeline.com.
If you like this book and would like to see what else we publish, please write, call, or E-mail us for our catalog.

Kanter's legal humor books are available at special bulk-purchase discounts for gifts, promotions, and fund-raising.
For details, contact Catbird Press.

Our books are distributed to the trade
by Independent Publishers Group.

To you "non-lawyers,"
who remind us lawyers what
"real life" is like.

Contents

Frae Monie a Blunder 7
Was That a *Tax* Lawyer Who Just
    Flew Over? 9
Forming the Flock 15
Ten Bucks Off 21
Leave No Valve Unturned 26
A Behind-the-Bars Look at the Bar 31
Art Over-Imitating Reality 37
Taking a Shine to You 44
Diary of An In-House Lawyer 49
Pressing for Information 55
Trial, By Juror 61
Lawyer:English Dictionary 68
Setting the Ground Rules 74
Talking About the Law 80
Total Quality Overmanagement 86
Legal Lemon Aid 91
Think I'll Make Me A Lawyer or Two 97
'Round the World 102
Conflicting Advice 111
In-House or Out-House 116
Oyez, O-No 122
Divorce, American Style 127
Philosophically Speaking 133
Ferreting Out What's Fair 138
Just a Formality 145

Out on the Beat   *152*
Of Sound Mind and Body   *157*
Surveying the Situation   *163*
What's Eating You, Anyway?   *169*
There's No Place Like . . .   *176*
The Devil Is In The Details   *181*
Habeas Corpus, For a Price   *187*
A Risky Proposition   *194*
Agent for Good   *199*
Playing It By The Numbers   *204*
Lovely To Look At   *209*
Trading Places   *218*
Postscript   *224*

Frae Monie a Blunder

LAST JULY THE FAIRWEATHER, WINTERS & SOMMERS firm threw itself a bash at the Bigwig Club to celebrate its fiftieth anniversary. In searching for a keynote speaker for the black tie dinner dance, the firm solicited suggestions from all its lawyers. Although the names floated in response to that solicitation included prominent politicians, entertainers, sports stars and academics, the overwhelming choice of the lawyers—as exemplified by the ballot of Stanley J. Fairweather, which read "Me"—was the firm's founder.

Fortunately, Stanley was available for the assignment and delivered an address that long will be remembered by those in attendance. The full text of his remarks is set forth below:

> Friends:
>
> It is a great privilege to welcome you.
>
> I requested the honor of speaking to you tonight for two reasons. First, I could think of no more appropriate speaker for the occasion. And second, I could think of no more certain way to assure that I would not be bored by some long-winded speech.
>
> I have decided that our fiftieth anniversary should be commemorated by an appropriate publication. Since I have written a memo explaining my choice for what that publication should be, and since all of you read, I see no reason to recite the memo to you.
>
> So now, in closing, I invite you to drink in moderation, dance with abandon and celebrate with joy.

Then Stanley circulated the following memo:

To: All
From: Stanley J. Fairweather
Re: Fiftieth Anniversary Book

    Thus far, the books that have been written about our firm have been rather insular. The first two, *The Handbook of Law Firm Mismanagement* and *Advanced Law Firm Mismanagement*, looked at lawyers from the point of view of lawyers, which is never particularly illuminating. The third, *The Ins & Outs of Law Firm Mismanagement*, was written from the point of view of our firm's staff, and so its perspective was necessarily limited.

    I think there is a compelling reason to venture outside the bounds of lawyers and those who work for our firm. As the Scottish poet, Robert Burns, wrote in his 1786 poem "To a Louse":

> *Oh wad some power the giftie gie us*
> *To see oursels as others see us!*
> *It wad frae monie a blunder free us,*
> *An' foolish notion.*

    Lawyers have no better giftie than other professions to see oursels as others see us. Some would say less. And it's the lack of that giftie which has led to so much of the foolishness that's been chronicled in the three previous books.

    On the occasion of our fiftieth anniversary, I have decided that we should invite the commentary of people outside our firm, to try to help us to see oursels as others see us. I have thus commissioned a book to be written by a wide range of outsiders who run into our firm in one way or another.

    It's even possible that the fruits of this effort will frae monie a blunder free us. But I sorta dute it.

    The fruits follow.

Was That a <u>Tax</u> Lawyer Who Just Flew Over?

Here's how it all started. One day, I was out in the marsh looking for heron, and I said to myself, "Louise, you've been standing out here in this marsh now for well over three hours. You're very chilly, your nose is running and you haven't seen a single heron. Just how long do you plan to stay out here doing this, anyway?" Well, since I'd put the question in that way, I left myself little choice but to answer, "I'm not going to stay out here a moment longer, Louise. I'm going to head home, get into some warm house slippers and fix myself a hot toddy."

It was over that hot toddy that I began to take stock of what had become of my life. Actually, it was over my third hot toddy, as I recall, that I really got into it. "Louise," I said to myself, "you're fifty-seven years old now, you've got a good job selling commercial real estate, your husband died two years ago, your children are grown, you own your own home in the suburbs, you enjoy reading historical romance novels and quilting tablecloths, you just had your hair cut short and tinted red, and what do you do, you spend all of your free time standing out in the marshes looking for water fowl."

"No," I corrected myself, "you're fifty-two years old, your job is in the audit department of a bank, you never married, you rent an apartment in the heart of downtown, you read only trashy mystery novels and you haven't changed your hair style or color since you were seventeen.

The only thing you got right is the part about the water fowl." It was then, in an epiphany, that I realized I had been looking for water fowl too darn long.

This realization, though, put me squarely on the horns of a dilemma. While I was sick and tired of searching for water fowl, I still enjoyed the voyeuristic pleasure of looking at things that are not aware I am looking at them. Also, I had just made an enormous investment in equipment—a high-powered telescope, a fancy single lens reflex camera with 500mm lens, bird call whistles, camouflage outfits and more. I was not willing to jettison all of that paraphernalia.

So I began to think of alternatives. I could decide to focus on big game, arrange safaris to far-flung parts of the globe. But those trips would stretch my budget beyond its breaking point. Also, who was I kidding? I'd be scared to death out there tracking rhinos.

Just then, as luck would have it, the phone rang. "Who was it on the phone?" you're probably wondering. I'll tell you in a moment, but first I need to set the stage.

About a year and a half ago, I got a letter from the IRS informing me that they were going to audit my tax return. Well, I nearly died. I started to think about all of the things they'd get me for. Probably I'd valued the sweaters and bras I'd given to the Salvation Army at somewhat more than their fair market value. Worse, I wasn't sure I had receipts for all of the business meals I'd deducted. So I figured they'd probably send me up the river for five to ten, minimum.

Luckily, though, unlike some people, I had a cousin Seymour to call. Seymour Plain is a tax partner at the Fairweather, Winters & Sommers law firm. Through clever representation and bargaining with the IRS, Seymour got me off with only a six-month prison term. No, only kidding; I went scot-free.

Yes, the phone call was from cousin Seymour. Seymour was very excited. For twenty-seven years he had toiled in anonymity as a tax lawyer at the Fairweather firm. Well, actually, he wasn't exactly anonymous; everyone knew he was Seymour, just plain Seymour (the irony of that characterization, given Seymour's surname, was not lost on lawyers at the firm).

But Seymour was calling to say that now, at last, he'd arrived. One of his senior partners, James Q. Sommers, had been called to an important meeting, with his maker. And, though Seymour was grief-stricken at James's passing, his loss had been ameliorated by the knowledge that he would inherit the departed's corner office. In fact, Seymour informed me, he was calling from his new office right that minute and was looking right down at my apartment building.

I asked Seymour which corner he was looking from, and he informed me that it was the northeast. I told him to hold on for a minute, dashed into my bedroom to grab my telescope and tripod, and raced into the living room to set it up. A moment later I returned to the phone and told cousin Seymour that I loved the blue-and-white-striped shirt he was wearing, with his initials on the pocket. Needless to say, Seymour was dumbfounded.

After we hung up, I went back to the living room to collect the telescope, but could not resist peeking through the lens again. At first, I looked just at my cousin, but then nudged the lens a bit to look at the woman in the office next to his. She was dressed in a conservative blue dress, with white buttons down the front and a white collar. On her walls, in addition to her law school diploma (Duke, '79, magna cum laude), were some finger paintings done by her children (Anita, 5, and Brian, 7). Papers were strewn all across her desk. Her secretary sat with a steno book in her hand, taking dictation, as the woman lawyer paced back and forth, first looking down at her feet and then glancing up and around at her secretary.

Almost involuntarily, I shifted the telescope to the next office. There sat a gentleman, a shelf full of big black volumes behind him with the names of corporations involved in public offerings and mergers embossed in gold on the spines. He wore a brown suit, had his wing-tipped shoes propped up on the desk, hands clasped behind his full head of graying hair, and appeared to be talking, though nobody else was in the room with him. His diploma showed him to be a graduate of Northwestern University School of Law, 1967, cum laude, and other certificates, hung in matching walnut frames on his wall, evidenced his admission to practice before the Supreme Court of the United States and the United States Tax Court, and his commendation for having served as Chair of the Tax Law Committee of the local bar association for sixteen years. He had to swing his feet off the desk occasionally in order to reach a white meerschaum pipe that sat in an ash tray on his desk.

I went back into my bedroom and searched for the notebook I took with me on my birding trips, then returned to the living room and began to write, glancing from time to time into the telescope:

> *Brown-suited, wing-tip-shoed, male tax lawyer, Northwestern '67. Cum. Partner. Pipe-smoker variety. Sighted with feet on desk, talking into speaker phone.*

I swung the telescope back to the woman in the office next to my cousin Seymour and noted in my book:

> *Blue-dressed, white-collared, female litigator, Duke '79. Magna. Partner. Messy-desked pacing dictator. Child-bearing.*

Excitedly, I shifted the telescope to the next office, where I spotted my first associate, eating a sandwich, his

shoes off, scratching the back of his head and flipping crumpled balls of paper over his shoulder into a waste basket. Quickly, I made more notes.

I was hooked.

Lawyer-watching has proved the answer to all my problems. I can do it in different places and ways, using the naked eye in the courtroom (binoculars elicit disapproving looks from the bench), and my telescope or binoculars for long-range observation. I photograph them in their natural habitats (which, of course, vary considerably, from elegant large firm offices to legal aid hovels) and at play. As I become a more practiced observer, I can identify and classify the lawyer I'm seeing simply by the way he moves (litigators walk quickly, ERISA lawyers amble about slowly) or holds his head (executive committee members elevate their noses, real estate lawyers watch the ground). Shoes, briefcases, hats, glasses—they all hold clues to proper identification.

And the varieties of lawyers seem endless. I already have more than two hundred on my life list.

Forming the Flock

"CAN WE PLEASE come to order?"
"Pass the mustard, please."
"Hey, who gave you the right to chair. . ."
"We need a name."
"Do we have a quorum?"
"I didn't get a copy of the agenda."
"I'll trade you, the mustard for the pickles."
"May I please have your attention for a minute."
"I bet you'll need more than a minute."

Surprisingly, the above dialogue is not taken from the transcript of a Fairweather, Winters & Sommers Executive Committee meeting. Instead, it emanates from a small group of Fairweather clients convened in the board room of Rite-Stuff Manufacturing Co., one of the firm's long-time clients. The meeting was called by Jack Rite, who was struggling to open the meeting.

"Ladies and gentlemen, please," Jack pleaded as the group finally quieted down. "Thank you all for coming. As I think you all know, my name is Jack Rite. Most of us have seen each other at the bimonthly ERISA seminars, bowling parties and weenie roasts the Fairweather firm has been hosting over the past several years in an attempt to purchase our loyalty. It's been so nice getting to know some of you that I thought it might be fun for us to get together without anybody from the Fairweather firm sidling up to us. So now that we're together, let's talk about what we would all like to see happen with this little group."

"I'd like to see our little group expand into a big group," said Rebecca Fissure, senior vice president and general counsel of Cellular Solutions, a biotechnology company.

"Yes, the firm has hundreds, even thousands of clients; I would think we ought to be able to attract more than seven," added Byron Fair, president of Fair Toxi-Beaut Corporation, and Stanley Fairweather's nephew.

"On the other hand, we assistant vice presidents at The First National Bank of Suburbia have found that a small group does have certain advantages," commented Ann-Louise Rutherford.

"Yes, if we are going to be—how shall I say it—discreet, it might be very advantageous to remain small," added Sheik Hamurabi Ben-Sulitan Mohammed Fasil Ben-Ayatola Holomon IV, who had engaged the Fairweather firm in several sensitive international legal matters.

"What do we need to be discreet for, Ben-Ben?" asked Rebecca.

"You can never tell. A sheep in the wilderness may still attract foxes."

"What's that supposed to mean?" asked Leonard Jenkins, a former futures trader who presently found himself on the streets.

"It's a saying in my country that illustrates the need for even a sheep in the wilderness to remain discreet."

"Why?"

"Well, for example, if it wore a pungent perfume, then, even in the wilderness, a sheep might attract a fox."

"A sheep wearing perfume?"

"It is only a saying."

"I see," said Leonard. "Frankly, the size of our group makes no difference to me. Big, small, who cares? As long as there's food at these shindigs, you can count me in."

"Doesn't the size of group we want depend on what we're trying to accomplish?" asked Jack.

"I suppose it does," said Rebecca. "I'd like to see a forum for us clients to get together to discuss problems we may have."

"That sounds like a good idea to me," said Byron. "I've been having a lot of trouble with my lower back lately. I get up, I feel fine; but around three in the afternoon I'm in agony."

"You should try swimming a couple times a week, Byron. That's terrific for your back. And leg lifts," advised Ann-Louise.

"You mean like this?" asked Byron, getting down on the floor and lifting both legs apart at a 45-degree angle. "Ooh, that hurts."

"No, cross them and lift them together, arch your lower back so that it's flat against the floor."

"Wait a minute, that isn't exactly the type of problem I was thinking of," said Rebecca. "I mean what about the ridiculous way Fairweather's legal fees have been going through the roof lately! And then, on top of it, I get charged $.25 a page for photocopying, $2 a page to send a fax and $25 for the two tuna sandwiches we ate in a conference at the firm. Those are the things that concern me."

"Thanks a lot, Rebecca. You don't give a damn about my back, do you?"

"It's not that, Byron, it's just that I don't think there's any particular reason to think that this group will be able to deal with that problem."

"There's a pretty good reason, actually. I was a physical therapist before I went to work for the bank," announced Ann-Louise.

"Well, yes, but that's just an accident."

"Like heck it was. I went to physical therapy school for two years. Was it just an accident that you went to law school, Rebecca?"

"I'm sorry, I didn't mean to offend you, Ann-Louise. I meant that it was coincidental that we happened to have an expert in our group who was able to deal with Byron's back problem—which I really do care about—and. . ."

"I have this really terrible kink in my neck that I get from time to time," said Ben-Ben. "Sometimes I can hardly turn my head."

"Just close your eyes and move your head slowly from side to side, like this, stretching gently, five times to each side. Then, when you're through with that, rotate your head clockwise ten times, then counterclockwise ten times, very slowly, like this. Then drop your head forward, gently, and slowly bring it all the way back. That's it. Try that for a week or so and if it doesn't feel better, call me at the bank. Here's my card."

"Actually, I think it feels a little better already," said Ben-Ben, who had been following along with Ann-Louise as she demonstrated the neck exercises.

"Look, I hate to interrupt," said Rebecca, "but I thought what we had in common was not our physical ailments, but that we all were clients of the Fairweather firm. It seems to me that we should focus the group's activities on what brings us together, in other words, the Fairweather link," said Rebecca.

"That certainly is what I had in mind. For example, this total quality management stuff they babble about constantly is driving me nuts," admitted Jack.

"Sounds okay to me," added Leonard, "but I think we need a name."

"What do you mean?" asked Byron.

"Our group. I think we need a name."

"Would it not be better to remain nameless?" asked Ben-Ben.

"No, I think we need a name," insisted Leonard.

"Okay, but let's make it something. . ."

"Discreet?" suggested Byron.

"Yes."

"How about The Secret Society of the Scented Sheep?" offered Rebecca.

"That's not funny," said Ben-Ben. "I was thinking of something like The Committee for Democracy in Government."

"But that has nothing to do with what we're about," objected Jack.

"Of course not. *That's* what makes it discreet."

"How about something a little more straightforward, like The Fairweather Clients Association?" suggested Byron.

"Perfect," said Leonard.

"Unless anybody has a problem with that, let's agree to that name," said Jack. "And it's getting pretty late, so why don't we adjourn now and meet in a month, back here, if everybody is still interested in continuing this."

"I certainly am. I think it's been a great meeting," said Ann-Louise. "I can tell that this group is going to have tremendous impact."

"How can you possibly tell that?" asked Leonard.

"It has already. I'm thinking of leaving the bank and going back into physical therapy."

"Well, that's wonderful, Ann-Louise," said Jack. "But I think maybe we could move this group along a bit faster if we formed a subcommittee to consider some of the things we may face, going forward, so I'm going to ask Rebecca, Ben-Ben and Leonard to serve as that subcommittee. We've made good progress today. After all, we already have a name."

"Actually, I'm not sure we can use that name," said Rebecca. "There's nobody called Fairweather in our group. We might be violating the firm's rights by using that name."

"No problem," said Byron. "I'll check it out. I'll call Uncle Stanley for a legal opinion."

Ten Bucks Off

I'M SO PROUD OF HER. My daughter, Sharon. She's a lawyer. She went to law school and everything. You have to do that to be a lawyer, but I'm not sure why. Because now, after four years of college and three years of law school, she's *practicing*. This I don't exactly understand. After all that time, you'd think maybe she could do it already, not just practice, but what do I know? Not much, I'll tell you.

When I grew up, Sharons weren't lawyers. Sharons were mothers, Sharons were nurses and maybe Sharons were teachers. Today it's all different. Sharons can be anything. And this is good, I think. Opportunity today knocks. I didn't have such knocking.

You should see my Sharon's office. The other day, I went to visit her. I almost got a nosebleed. Two elevators you have to take. One is not good enough. And I walk off of the elevator and this beautiful young lady is sitting behind flowers that must have cost somebody $300, such a bouquet. I wasn't sure they were real 'til I went over and pinched them.

And this lady behind the flowers asks me whom do I want to see. And I tell her Sharon. And she says, "Oh, do you mean Ms. Kelcher?" Yes, I tell her. "And whom may I say is calling?" she asks me. And I tell her that the whom whom is calling is Sharon's mother, also Ms. Kelcher. So formal they are with their whoms and Mses and flowers.

I'm one of Sharon's best customers. When I see her, I always grab a bunch of those darling little cards she has printed up, with her name and phone number on it. And the name of her firm. It's the Goodweather something and something firm, I don't remember exactly, but they make a squiggly little sign before the last something, not an "and." And I give these little cards out to everyone I know, and I tell them to call Sharon if they have any problems. So who doesn't have problems these days? So my Sharon, she gets lots of calls.

But she's not so happy about all of the calls she gets, my Sharon. She says some of my friends call her and complain that their husbands are good-for-nothings. This, she points out to me, is not a legal problem. Men are good-for-nothings; this is a problem of nature. I agree with her here. She says that she asks the women who call about their husbands if they want to consider a divorce, but they all tell Sharon no, that a good man is hard to find; and I agree with this, too.

So Sharon says all of these calls she gets because I pass out her cards in certain places—like the other day I must've given out fifty in line at the movies—are not doing her any good, and I should stop giving them out. Here we get into an argument. "I'm not supposed to help my daughter?" I ask.

"You can help me, Mama, but what I'm trying to tell you is that passing my cards out to everyone you meet just means I get a whole lot of phone calls that take up a lot of my time, but don't bring in any business. People call me up with all of their personal problems. They think I'm Ann Landers."

So this was news to me, frankly. I thought a lawyer solves problems. What do I know what's a legal problem and what's a problem for Ann Landers? I read the newspapers, I see that people are suing left and right to solve all of their problems, and collecting millions of dollars because they spill hot coffee on themselves—they should soon my Sharon tells me she's getting a bunch of calls from people who really want some legal services, what did I do? Naturally, I don't say anything to her.

Then, a few months later, she starts sending out her bills and she gets my cards back, with the ten dollar discount, and she calls me up and she's plenty upset. So I ask her, would she rather have no business at $150 an hour or a lot of business at $140 an hour. She's still pretty hot under the collar until one day her senior partner, Stanley Goodweather, comes in and congratulates her, and tells her that her discount on the back of business cards idea is the first smart use he's seen of business cards in the fifty years he's been passing them out, and he's having the discount notice printed on the back of all firm business cards. So now Sharon doesn't think that her mama's so dumb.

So it's nice that Sharons can be lawyers these days, especially my Sharon. But I don't think that I would have been a lawyer, even if I had the opportunity, to tell you the truth, though. I mean it's all so complicated—the rules, the language, what you do in court, all of the papers you have to fill out. Sure, you have fancy offices, two elevators, big bouquets of flowers, business cards, and they call you "whom" and "Ms." But, I mean, when you get right down to it, who needs it?

Leave No Valve Unturned

PRIOR TO MEETING HIS ATTORNEY, Harold Punctillio, Jack Rite, president of Rite-Stuff Manufacturing Company, sent Harold a proposed letter agreement with Rite-Stuff's long-time supplier Ace Valve Corp., which read:

Fred Jencks
Ace Valve Corp.
549 Fulton Ave.
New York, NY 10043

Dear Fred:
    This will confirm that you're going to continue to supply us with number 14 valves for our model 86 framing machines at a price of $.32 per valve. Sign if you agree.
    Best to Sally.

                        Sincerely,

                        Jack Rite

    The conversation below took place at Pete's Bar, to which Jack retired with his vice-president, Gladys Acstone, after meeting for three hours with Harold about the proposed letter agreement.

    "I didn't know you drank martinis," Jack said when Gladys ordered a double vodka martini, extra dry.

    "I don't, normally. Only after meetings with Harold."

    "He was in some form today, wasn't he."

    "I'll say. I knew we were in trouble when he said he 'just had a few comments' and then asked if we had any early dinner plans."

"Do you have your notes, so we can review what he said?"

"Yes. First he asked us what a number 14 valve was, and we told him that the number 14 valve controlled the flow of oil to the motor. Harold suggested that Ace could make a new valve and call it number 14, but we said that as long as it fits our model 86, we didn't care. Harold noted that our letter neglected to say that the number 14 valve had to fit. We recognized Harold's point, but said that we could easily alter the letter to cover that.

"Harold pointed out that the new valve 14 might fit, but not perform its function. We asked Harold why Fred would do a thing like that. Harold allowed as how he didn't even know Fred, so he couldn't really say why Fred might do that, but that he had seen people do strange things, and that's what lawyers are for. We assured Harold that Fred would not do something crazy.

"Harold suggested that perhaps we should have a provision in our letter that required that Fred not do anything crazy, and giving us the right to terminate the agreement if he did. That provision might also provide for specific performance or liquidated damages in the event that Fred did do something crazy. We asked how we would know if something Fred did was 'crazy.' Harold said we'd have to define crazy in the agreement, and that it would probably be wise to provide for arbitration in the event the parties could not agree as to whether what Fred had done was crazy.

"We wondered who the arbitrators would be to determine this—psychiatrists? Harold said no, that we were not talking about 'crazy' in the psychological sense. At this point Harold launched into a description of the different types of crazy in the law, including the prerequisite state of mind to commit a crime, what would be required to institutionalize somebody, and crazy in the business sense, which he said means something that a jury would determine that an ordinarily prudent business person would not do.

"Harold said that he personally favored a provision for three arbitrators, each party to select one and those two to select the third, though, of course, a procedure would have to be spelled out and provision made in the event that one of the parties failed to appoint its arbitrator. We would also have to specify who would pay the cost of arbitration, where the arbitration would take place and which law would govern. Harold recommended the law of Nebraska."

At this point, Gladys ordered another vodka martini, extra dry.

"Your notes are excellent," said Jack. "Why don't you continue."

"Okay, then Harold asked what happened if we changed our model 86. We pointed out that we'd been using that model just as it is, with minor modifications, for thirty years. We added that we didn't anticipate any changes, but if we were to, Fred would just have to make parts to fit it.

"At that point, Harold interrupted to say, 'Aha, but the agreement doesn't say that, does it?'

"We admitted that it did not, but said that we assumed that if we changed the machine, Fred, of course, would make parts to fit the new machine.

"*Crazy* Fred?" asked Harold.

"We said that, well, if Fred didn't make parts to fit the new machine, we supposed we would just have to find ourselves a new supplier. But Harold opined that we might not have the right to do that, since the letter we had proposed to send Fred might be construed to require us to buy all of our requirements from Fred.

"We said that we would then just not call the new machine a model 86; we'd come up with a catchy new name, like 'model 87.' But Harold said that Fred might be able to argue that we subverted the intent of the agreement by changing the model number of our machine and sue us, claiming damages equal to our profits over a period of years, assuming an increase in sales of ten or fifteen percent per annum, and perhaps even seeking punitive damages for our fraudulent effort to avert the clear intent of the letter agreement.

"We asked Harold what kind of clear intent he was referring to, since by then we'd been talking for over an hour about what the letter meant, and that the only thing that was absolutely clear was that the letter was not clear. Harold, however, said that, after considering its meaning for two or three months, the court would find its meaning clear and therefore he would recommend, at least, that we insert a provision in the letter specifying a maximum amount of damages we might be liable for."

"Oh yes, I remember that. Wasn't that when Harold launched into the question of what '$.32' meant?" asked Jack.

"Yes, he pointed out that there were dollars in Canada, Australia and several other countries, so that he thought it extremely dangerous to leave an ambiguity as to which sort of dollar we were talking about in the letter."

At this point, Gladys ordered her third double martini.

"Then he started asking about how long the agreement was to last, and what amount Fred would agree to supply of the valve, whether Fred could increase the price, what would happen in the event of a war, or a strike, or fire that prevented Fred from producing or us from using and then. . ."

"Yes, my head was spinning at that point, but I had to admit that Harold had a point: those things could go wrong. But he really lost me at the end," admitted Jack.

"You mean the part about Sally?"

"Yes, when he asked me what 'Best to Sally' meant."

"And you told him that this was intended to say hello to Fred's wife, but he cautioned that a court would seek to put some business meaning into it, since it was part of a contract. And you said 'Such as what?' and he said it might mean that the best number 14 valves were to go to Sally and there just might be a Sally Manufacturing Company that could use those valves. So he thought that might be a problem; one shouldn't leave these things to chance and, if we wanted, he could have one of his young associates research the question . . . Say, where are you going, Jack?"

"I'm going to call Fred, and tell him to send the valves."

A Behind-the-Bars Look at the Bar

CONVICTED CRIMINALS have their own view of the legal profession, as shown by the conversation below, taped in the federal prison in Ossining, New York.

"What're you in for?" asked Four-Fingers Hentschler.
"Arson. You?" replied Snooker Gallagher.
"Aggravated battery."
"I'm Herbert Hentschler, by the way. Folks call me Four-Fingers."
"Albert Gallagher, but I go by Snooker. Pleased to make your acquaintance," he said, reaching for Four-Fingers' hand.
"Charmed," replied Four-Fingers.
"You seem to have all your fingers on this hand," said Snooker, glancing down. "Did you lose one on the other hand?"
"Nope. Got em all."
"Then why do they call you Four-Fingers?"
"It's a long story."
"Well, I've got twenty years, what about you?"
"Same."
"Well, I reckon that'd be enough time for your story, ain't it?"
"Yup."
"Well?"
"Don't feel like tellin it, just now."

"Have it your way. This your first time?"

"Huh?"

"In the pen, first time?"

"Hell, no. My third. Do I look like some kinda rookie to ya?"

"Nope. I didn't mean no offense, just makin a little conversation."

"Yeh, well if I was you, Snooker, I wouldn't make so much conversation. That's what got me in here in the first place."

"Whaddaya mean?"

"The aggravated battery. It was because somebody wanted to talk to me more than I wanted to talk to somebody."

"How'd that come about?"

"I was talkin to my lawyer, well my ex-lawyer, over at Fairweather, Winters & Sommers."

"Bout what?"

"Bout lawyerin"

"What kinda lawyerin?"

"His lawyerin."

"What about it?"

"How I didn't think much of it."

"How come?"

"Cause it was his lawyerin sent me up the river for mail fraud."

"That what you were in for last time?"

"Last two times."

"They got you twice? Ain't that whatchamacallit . . . double trouble?"

"You mean double jeopardy?"

"Yeh, that's it. Ain't it that?"

"Not technicly."

"How come?"

"Cause the two mail fraud deals was ten years apart, and they was different deals altogether."

"Oh, too bad. What was they?"

"Well, the last one was for sellin coupon books that offered discounts at restaurants, clothing stores, furniture places and so forth, etcetra. I put together those books and offered em to people for fifty bucks. It was a terrific deal cause there was over $4,000 worth of coupons in em."

"And that's against the law?"

"Yup."

"How come?"

"Cause I didn't get no permission from the theaters and stores to put them coupons in my book."

"Oh, how come?"

"Oversight."

"Oversight?"

"Yup, that's what my lawyer, Harvey Holdem, argued."

"Didn't work, huh?"

"Not exactly, there was a problem."

"What was that?"

"Well, I'd been in the coupon book business a couple times before in other states and was caught at it."

"Oh, that's a problem, alright."

"You bet it was, got me sent up the river for two-to-four."

"So when you got out, you went to see your ex-lawyer?"

"Yep, paid Harvey a little visit and rearranged certain of his facial features a bit."

"And for that they got ya for aggravated battery?"

"Yup."

"How come aggravated?"

"Don't know, I guess because Harvey was pretty aggravated bout the way his face got rearranged."

"Who represented you in the battery case?"

"Well, I tried to get my ex to do it."

"Ya mean Harvey, the one who you beat the hell out of?"

"Yep."

"Why him?"

"Incentive."

"Whaddayamean incentive?"

"I figgur he's got a real incentive to do a good job for me, cause he seen what happened when he didn't do so good a job."

"What about the money you pay him, ain't that incentive?"

"Hell no it ain't, Snooker. Harvey gets paid that money whether I go up the river or not, so there ain't much incentive there, is there?"

"No, I guess not."

"Maybe there ought to be contingent criminal work, like for automobile accidents."

"Huh?"

"Well, you get hit by some drunk and you can get a lawyer who'll take yur case and collect only out of what you win. So his interest's the same as yours. Maybe we should get criminal lawyers to take cases and get paid only if they get you off the hook, or get paid only a little if you're convicted, but a lot if you walk."

"Sounds like a great idea to me, Four-Fingers."

"Thanks."

"But Harvey wouldn't take your case, huh?"

"Nope."

"How come?"

"Somethin 'bout 'conflict of interest'."

"What'd he mean?"

"Well, he said he'd be the chief witness for the state against me, so he didn't see how he could cross-examine hisself. Also, he said he wanted to see me put away for a good, long time."

"So what did you say to that?"

"I told him I wasn't worried about his cross-examination."

"Why not?"

"Two reasons. First, he's such a no-good, low-life sleaze-ball that nobody's gonna believe what he says, anyway. And second, I seen his cross-examination in my other case and it wasn't worth a damn, anyway."

"But what about his wantin to see you put away, ain't that a problem?"

"Not really. I told him that lawyers are called upon to represent unpoplar clients all the time, and that he oughta be able to separate out his own feelins about someone from his profeshnal duty to represent them to the best of his ability."

"Hey, that sounds pretty good, where did ya get that from?"

"School."

"What kinda school?"

"Law school."

"You mean you went to law school?"

"Yaa, but I didn't graduate."

"How come, too tough?"

"Hell no, too dumb."

"Whaddayamean too dumb?"

"Ya spend all day tryin to see forty different sides of every question, never doin nothin. Besides, after a little more than a semester, I got some good ideas and I was dyin to try em out."

"What kinda good ideas?"

"Well, the coupons for one."

"You mean the stuff you got sent up for, the mail fraud, you learned in law school?"

"Sure, the case books in law school are loaded with good ideas. It's just that the people who tried em out wasn't smart enough to pull em off, or just got unlucky. Doesn't mean they weren't great ideas."

"So you recommend law school as training for us aspirin criminals, Four-Fingers?"

"Absolutely. No matter what side of the law you want to wind up on, there's nothin like law school to get you there."

"I think you just came up with a great new marketin idea."

"What're ya talkin about?"

"Well, my lawyer was tellin me how the law schools are all cryin cause enrollment's gone way down. But they're just not tappin their market fully. They're missin all of us guys."

"That's right. And for us criminal element, law school should be a heckuva lot more attractive than for those other poor slobs who go."

"How come?"

"How come? You gotta be kiddin, just think of it—one semester instead of six, no pressure bout grades, no worries bout jobs after law school, no bar exam to look forward to, no fifty years of scroungin around for and bowin and scrapin at the feet of clients. . ."

"Four-Fingers, you're a genius."

"Uh-huh."

Art Over-Imitating Reality

TELEVISION PRODUCERS Hiram Freebish and Sally Rinsel were sitting around brainstorming one day (the way creative television producers do), and suddenly Sally was struck by a creative idea of the first magnitude. She signaled this to Hiram by saying, "Hey, Hiram, I've just been struck by a creative idea of the first magnitude."

Hiram looked at Sally, struck his forehead with the palm of his right hand, and said that he had been thinking the same thing himself. Sally questioned how that could be so, since she had not yet told Hiram what she had been thinking about. But Hiram insisted that whatever it was she had been thinking about, if it was an idea of the first magnitude he had been thinking it, too.

"Well, if that's the case," Sally challenged, "what is it that I was thinking about?"

"You were thinking about doing a television show based on corporate lawyers," Hiram opined.

And, indeed, Sally had. She had wondered why all of the many shows about lawyers featured trial lawyers.

Sally decided to talk to her cousin, Herbert Rinsel, who was a corporate associate at Fairweather, Winters & Sommers, about her idea. Herb, she knew, would tune in immediately. Not only was he a corporate lawyer, but Herb had also co-directed his high school variety show and had always regarded it as something of a waste that the law, instead of Hollywood, had snagged him. Sally was not disappointed. When she floated her idea to Herb, he struck his forehead with the palm of his right hand and allowed as how he had been thinking the same thing himself.

Though somewhat taken aback by the fact that everyone seemed to be thinking of her idea of the first magnitude, Sally nonetheless proposed to Herb that he take a shot at writing a pilot episode. Herb readily agreed and, after closeting himself for four weeks in the board room at Fairweather, Winters & Sommers, produced the following script (yet still managed to bill 250 hours to corporate clients):

The Deal Lawyers

Scene 1

(We are in the main conference room of a fancy law firm. The table is stacked high with documents. Portraits, presumably of the firm's founders, line the wood-paneled walls. Two half-empty coffee cups sit on the table. T. William Williams (known to his partners and clients as "T-Bills"), a tall, silver-haired man of about 55, surveys the scene and speaks to Lydia Milife, a comely blond woman of 32.)

T-Bills:
I can't believe the deal's going to close tomorrow.

Lydia:
No, me neither.

T-Bills:
Remember when this all started, about a year ago, at the meeting with our client Consolidated Separations?

Lydia:
No, I wasn't at that meeting.

T-Bills:
Oh, yes, that's right. But do you remember how I told you it started, about a year ago, at the meeting with our client Consolidated Separations?

Lydia:
Uh-huh.

Scene 2

(A flashback. We are in the office of T. William Williams. His desk is stacked high with documents. Portraits, presumably of the firm's founders, line his wood-paneled office. Two half-empty coffee cups sit on his desk. T. William Williams, a tall, silver-haired man of about 54, surveys the scene and speaks to J. B. Wilcox, a balding gentleman in his late sixties, wearing a blue suit and a red-and-green-striped bow tie, who is off-camera.)

T-Bills:
So, J.B., I guess I'd better get going on this merger you just told me all about in great detail and in a very interesting way. It's a complicated deal, that's for sure, and the time pressure is intense, but we at the Fairweather firm are noted for that type of steely-cool calm under fire. So, I should have a rough draft of that agreement for you within the next three weeks.

J.B. (from off camera)
Thanks T-Bills. I'll sure be looking forward to seeing it.

Scene 3

(We are back in the conference room where Scene 1 took place.)

T-Bills:
Yup, wasn't that a time?

Lydia:
Sure was.

T-Bills:
Remember how we worked together to get that thing done?

Scene 4

(We are back in T-Bills' office—documents stacked, photos of founders, etc.—this time with Lydia present.)

T-Bills:
And so, Lydia, that's the deal. J.B. and I are counting on you to draft one heck of a document. I suggest you try starting with our form merger agreement. And, if that doesn't work, you might try our form will, with pour-over trust and full marital.

Lydia:
Okay. When's he need it?

T-Bills:
No big rush, 'bout three weeks. *(Phone rings. T-Bills picks it up and speaks.)* Oh, hi, J.B . . . Yup, Lydia and I were just talking about how we were going to tackle your agreement . . . You do . . . Oh, I see . . . Sure, that should be no problem. *(Hangs up, and speaks to Lydia.)* Ah, Lydia, J.B. says he'll need that agreement in three days. *(Lydia faints.)*

Scene 5

(We are in Lydia's office. It is small and is not wood-paneled, but portraits, presumably of the founders, hang in the office. Two half-empty cups of coffee sit on her desk. She is working at her computer, as we watch her typing away furiously for several minutes.)

Lydia:
(Speaking to herself) There, that should just about do it. Now all I've got to do is print it out, get it up to proofreading, have it photocopied and then fax it over to J. B.'s office, wait for his comments, revise it, print it, get it up to proofreading, have it photocopied and messenger it out to the other side. Talk about exhilaration. It doesn't get a whole lot better than this. *(NOTE: preview for next segment should suggest that viewers will see how the other side reacts to receiving the first draft of the merger agreement, and find out where T-Bills is planning to go on vacation.)*

When Sally received Herb's pilot episode, she called him immediately to say it was the dullest thing she had ever read in her life. Herb protested that it was extremely realistic. Sally speculated that therein could lie the reason that we'd seen no previous shows about the lives of corporate lawyers. She pleaded with Herb to give it another try, and not to worry so much about the realism.

Herb is hard at work on another pilot, which starts as follows:

The Deal Lovers

Scene 1

(We are in the main conference room of a fancy law firm. The table is stacked high with documents. Portraits, presumably of the firm's founders, line the wood-paneled walls. Two half-empty coffee cups sit on the table. T. William Williams, a tall, silver-haired man of about 55, surveys the scene and speaks to Lydia Milife, a comely blond woman of 32.)

T-Bills:
(Breathing heavily) Oh, Lydia, Lydia.

Lydia:
(Breathing heavily) Oh, T-Bills, T-Bills.

T-Bills:
(Groping to unbutton her blouse.) Oh, Lydia.

Lydia:
(Groping to unsuspend his suspenders.) Oh, T-Bills.

T-Bills:
Oh.

Lydia:
Oh. But, but T-Bills . . . the closing.

T-Bills:
To hell with the closing, Lydia. Can't you see that ours is a merger that doesn't need Justice Department approval; you and I are dealing with a higher law, Lydia, a law of trust, not antitrust.

Lydia:
Oh, knock it off, T-Bills, you gorgeous hunk of corporate lawyer. . .

Taking a Shine to You

I SHINE SHOES. That's my bizness, Man. I shine 'em up, snap my rag, give my customers a little chatter, talk 'em up, dance 'round a little. I'm a profeshnal. I bring back the luster. And I entertain, too; yessir, I'm in the show bizness *and* the shoe bizness, both of 'em.

I'm what ya call a rovin' shoeshine man. I mainly work one big office buildin', goin' 'round and shinin' shoes, door to door, askin' folks do they need a shine or not. One of my big customers is the folks at the Fairweather law firm. I been shinin' them up since they moved inta my buildin', mebee twenty years ago. Do I have some stories? You bet I do, Man, you bet I do.

I'm not sure I should be tellin' them to you, 'cause I might be vilotatin' the lawyer/shoeshiner privlidge. You think I'm jokin'? Yeh, well mebee I am, but I'm tellin' you that if there ain't a lawyer/shoeshiner privlidge, there sure nuff oughta be—for the lawyer's sake. The things I heard, whew. I go inta their offices and they talk like I'm not there, or deaf or somethin', or like I don't understand English.

But you ain't gonna find me snitchin' on confidenshal stuff I heard. No sir. 'Cause some of them Fairweather guys bound to read this book, and if they get the idea I ain't trustworthy, there goes my bizness, out the winda. Yeh, bein' trustworthy's least as important in a shoeshine man as in a lawyer.

You sure do have a lot of difrent types of lawyers up there, I'll tell ya. Some of it's got ta do with age. I get a kick outa the young ones, the babies I call 'em, to maself. They see me walkin' by their offices, carryin' my parryfanalia and I'll ask 'em do they want a shine. And most of 'em they're embarrassed, and they look down and shake their heads no. And I'll tell 'em mebee tmorrow, and move on down the hall. Most new lawyers it'll take a year or more before they'll have me shine 'em up.

Sometimes it'll get started when they're in a partner's office and I'll come by and the partner'll call me in to do a shine when the young one's talkin' with him. And the partner'll ask the youngster does he want a shine, it'll be on him, the partner. So then the baby gets the idea that this is okay, and mebee he'll say yes. And the partner and youngster they'll be talkin' about some big corporate takeover or somethin', which, technicly, I ain't supposed ta be hearin'. Made me a little bit a money in the stock market that way. Nothin' big, though, 'cause I ain't no hog like them fancy lawyers and investment bankers you read about in the paper who're doin' time.

Anyways, mebee the next time I go by the young one's office he feels comfortable to invite me in for a shine. Now, it's funny to watch 'em the first couple times I do a shine. They don't know quite what to do with themselves. They can't just set there and do nothin'. And they don't want to talk to me, 'cause they're not too sure what to say, or whether I kin talk or not. So they'll just stare straight ahead for a while, not lookin' at nothin' and not doin' nothin'. But they realize that that ain't right, 'cause they wastin' good billable time. So they'll pick somethin' up offa their desk and start into readin' it.

Now I know they can't read nothin' cause they're too nervous and I'm sittin' there poppin' my rag and movin' 'round and adjustin' their shoe so I can get the right angle. But there they are, sittin' and pretendin' to read. And I'll bet if I asked 'em what the hell they read while I was shinin', not a one of 'em could tell me a bit of it. But least if they're readin' while I'm shinin', you can bet they're billin' it to their clients.

Heck, I don't blame 'em for being nervous. I remember back when I first started shinin', I was plenty nervous then, too. Takes a while for a profeshnal to get his confidence in any field, I guess. Some of 'em develop that confidence quicker than others.

Anyways, when you get one of them youngsters for a shine for the first time, it's fun to see what they do after it's over. Some ask me what they owe me. I usually tell 'em I'll settle for the same hourly rate they bill their clients, even though I'm a heckuva lot more experienced at what I do than they are at what they do. That gets a chuckle out of most of 'em, unless they went to a particularly fancy law school and don't know how ta laugh. Then most of 'em will ask what I really charge. I tell 'em it's three bucks, but I can let 'em have it for a buck fifty a shoe, if they prefer. It's my way of alternative billin'.

Anyways, as those associates spend a few years there, I see which of 'em talks to me and which ones pretend I'm not there. I see which ones treat me like a person who kin talk and think and feel, and which ones seem to think they too good for me.

Some of them talk to me about my specialty, shoes. That's all right, I know somethin' 'bout that. They want to know which are the best kind to buy, which are better, rubber or leather heels, how do you care for 'em so's to get the most life outa them. But the ones who I *know* are gonna make it are the ones who ask me about what I notice in my work at the firm, what's changed over the years I've been shinin', what I expect's comin' down the road, that sorta thing. That's the kinda conversations me and Stanley always have.

Fact is, I kin do a pretty darn good job of predictin' which of the young folks are goin' to make it to the Fairweather Executive Committee, and who ain't. How do I know I can do that? Well, I made me a bit of money on it. Me and Stanley Fairweather, we got a bettin' system set up on us predictin' who's gonna become a Executive Committee member and who's not. You surprised that me and Stanley bet together? Well, him and me, we're pretty close. You get that way when you shine a man's shoes twice a week for twenty years.

Now I got some unfair advantages over Stanley in pickin', I'll admit. He's got to go by the reports he gets from his partners on how good the associate's work is, and he picks his picks on who's gonna make it to the Executive Committee on those reports. The people who're makin' those reports can see if that associate can write and think like a lawyer. And that may get them to become a partner. But I get to see how those associates behave, and that's how clients see 'em. And the way they *behave* is what decides whether they gonna become really successful partners or not, not the kinda legal work they do.

Heck, all of 'em all is plenty smart 'nuff to be a lawyer. Mebee some of 'em is a little smarter than some others, but not nuff to make no big difference. Some of them, though, is a lot more able to behave like human be-ins, and that's what makes the real diffrence. That's what keeps clients coming back, that's what brings in the dough and that's what puts people on the Executive Committee.

Heck, same thing's true with my bizness. There's plenty people's got the technique and intelligence to shine a fella's shoes, and I don't mean to be braggin' here, but not everyone's got my style, if you know what I mean. Heck, if I wasn't so modest, I'd say I was definitely Executive Committee material.

Yup, me and Stanley, we've talked 'bout a lot a things over the years. In fact, I think I mighta been the one first got Stanley thinkin' seriously 'bout how women were gonna mean some big changes. He told me how they weren't gonna treat women no diffrent than men. I told him that that don't make no sense. I explained how from my profeshnal point of view, the comin' of lady lawyers was the biggest change I seen. At first they weren't inclined to use my services at all, and their shoe styles presented severe polishing challenges for those of us in the trade. Over time, though, as they became a more significant factor in the shinin' market, I developed methods of handlin' them problems. I don't think the law firm's done quite so well with ladies, mebee 'cause they think they're same as men.

And I hear a lot about folks' personal problems, too, especially the partners'. You might not think they'd talk to the shoeshine man 'bout those things. But, fact is, for some of 'em I'm the only one they can talk to. They work so hard they got no family. And they can't talk to their partners, 'cause that shows they're weak. Yup, I heard 'bout a lot of broken dreams in my day. I'm a good listener; that's part of the service I provide. And it's usually worth a nice tip.

So, in genral, I got no big problem with the folks at the Fairweather firm. Sure, a few of 'em got the idea that their shoes don't need no ground to walk on. But I don't lay that off on them bein' lawyers; I lay that off on them bein' people. Some folks just gotta feel like they're a little better than the next guy. But I know diffrent. Sittin' on a little stool all day lookin' at people's feet . . . well, it sorta levels folks out for ya.

Diary of An In-House Lawyer

REBECCA FISSURE, an associate at the Fairweather firm, left to join the legal department of Cellular Solutions, a biotechnology company and a firm client. Below are selected excerpts from Becky's diary, which begin shortly before she left the firm.

December 8, 1992. I feel like something of a failure. It's not exactly that I *have* to leave the firm. They didn't tell me that. But in my review last week, Phil Wilson said that there were doubts as to whether I was "partnership material," whatever that means. It's not going to be easy leaving the firm, after five years, but I think it's the best thing for me.

Phil told me that his client, Cellular Solutions, who I was doing some work for, was looking for somebody to start an in-house legal department. Working for a legal department seems like a big step down in prestige. And I would have to take a rather substantial salary cut, but we'd be able to survive okay, because my husband, Joe, makes a pretty good salary. I would get some stock options from Cellular, but who knows whether those will ever be worth anything. Phil said he'd be happy to recommend me for the post, if I were interested. I told him to go ahead and put my name in.

December 15, 1992. Word has gotten around the associate ranks that I may be leaving the firm, and lots of people have been coming by to wish me well. Most of them actually seem to be a bit jealous that it's me, and not them, who is leaving the firm. Several of them have told me that if the work gets to be too much for me, to keep them in mind wherever I go. I'm sure going to miss things around here.

December 16, 1992. Offered job at CS. Accept it immediately.

December 17, 1992. The firm threw me a going-away party this afternoon, in the large conference room. Several partners spoke, including Sherman Clayton, who called me "Renee." Garrison Phelps told me not to pay any attention to that, since after twenty-two years as his partner, Sherman still refers to him as "Harry."

Two young partners took me aside to tell me that if there was any legal work they could help me with, I should feel free to call them directly, rather than bothering Phil Wilson with every little detail.

Phil made a nice speech, saying what a fine lawyer I was and how much the firm would miss me. I resisted asking him why, if this were so, I wasn't "partnership material." Phil took me aside to let me know that he'd be happy to act as the clearing house for any legal work that I send to the firm.

Stanley Fairweather presented me with a gift from the firm, a leather portfolio with my initials embossed on the front. He took me aside to ask me if Phil had requested that I direct all legal work through him. When I said that Phil had, Stanley said to ignore that and to direct the work wherever I damn pleased.

December 19, 1992. My last day in the office, as I plan to take the rest of the year off before starting at CS. Went around to say goodbyes to my friends. Three young partners told me that if I should need help, I should keep them in mind for the CS legal department.

Cleaned out my office and found three watches and two fountain pens I'd been looking for for over two years. Packed up all of the large compilations of deals I worked on into eight cardboard boxes, each weighing approximately two hundred pounds. These books will line the shelves of my new office at CS, and will remain unopened as they have here at the firm.

January 4, 1993. Started at CS today. Seems strange not having halls lined with attorneys, but it's not all bad. My new office is as big as Stanley Fairweather's.

Went out to lunch with a couple officers from CS and we actually discussed something other than the latest case or deal. In time, I may be able to adjust to this.

Phil Wilson sent over a lovely bunch of flowers. Thoughtful of him. When I called to thank him, he invited me out to lunch at the Bigwig Club next week. That's the first time I'll have been to lunch at the Bigwig since I was a summer associate six years ago, and the first time Phil's asked me out, ever. I'm sure it's a coincidence that it happens as I become a potential client. Probably he's been meaning to do it for a long time, anyway.

At the end of the day, I felt something strange as I got ready to leave. I tried to think why I was feeling that way. Suddenly it struck me—no time sheets. Can you imagine: I no longer have to account for every sixth of an hour I spend for the rest of my life. Ah, freedom.

January 6, 1993. A small item appeared in the *Tribune* about my new position, and I received calls from six of my law school classmates at other large firms, congratulating me and inviting me to lunch. Two of them asked whether I'd be needing any additional members of the CS legal department.

I unpacked all of the compilations and put them up on bookshelves. But when I got them up there, I decided that five years of staring at those damn things is enough, so I put them all back in the boxes, called Hurry Lopes at the Fairweather mailroom and asked him to send somebody over to collect the boxes. I'm having the bookshelves taken down and I'm going to put up some artwork that my daughter drew in kindergarten.

By the way, my daughter seems to love my new job. I've been home two evenings in a row, and she's helped me prepare dinner. She says that her daddy cooks better, though. She's right. Joe's had a lot more practice.

January 11, 1993. Lunched with Phil Wilson today at the Bigwig. Turns out he's actually quite a friendly and interesting guy. It's a shame associates at the firm never get a chance to see that side of him. I told that to Phil, suggesting that he might want to try treating the associates that worked with him as if they were clients. That notion sort of shocked old Phil, but he said he'd take it under advisement.

Towards dessert, Phil asked whether there might be any legal work that the firm could help me with. I told him that there were several lawsuits that the firm was already working on, and that I was in the process of reviewing their status and would want to meet with the lawyer in charge of each case to get their assessments as to likely outcome and the cost of continuing to litigate.

Phil thought that was an excellent idea and offered to sit in with me on those meetings. I thanked Phil, but told him that I didn't think it would be necessary to bother him with those meetings, unless he did not think those in charge were capable of handling the matters. He assured me that he had full confidence in those running the cases, and that perhaps I would like to save the additional cost of his participation in the meetings. I admitted that the thought had crossed my mind.

February 25, 1993. I called Phil to tell him that CS was considering acquiring another company and that I thought I would need outside counsel in handling the acquisition. Phil fairly bubbled with enthusiasm and suggested that I come over later that afternoon so that we could get started right away. I told Phil that I thought that might be a bit premature since I had prepared a brief summary of the transaction and would be requesting bids for handling the matter from four law firms, including the Fairweather firm.

After a long silence, Phil said that he understood and would be happy to bid on the matter. He pointed out, though, that his firm brought considerable value to the table, having represented CS since its inception and therefore being familiar with its business. I told him that I recognized that and had asked the other firms who were bidding to estimate how long it would take them to review the company's business and that I planned to ask each of them to absorb that time as an investment in a new client. Phil said that he thought that was a very wise approach on my part and commented upon how I appeared to be growing into the corporate counsel position very quickly. I thanked Phil.

He began reminiscing about how far he and I went back together, and all. I told him that I didn't think that would matter in my selection of counsel. He said he was sorry that it wouldn't, but that he could understand why, and all. He suggested we do lunch again sometime soon, since it had been quite a while. I told him that I didn't think it had been all that long, but that I would be happy to get together for lunch with him, as I'd like to catch up with what was going on at the firm.

March 18, 1993. I'm going to be working with Phil on our new acquisition. We've negotiated a maximum fee, and the hourly rates for each of the attorneys who will be working on the matter. At first Phil resisted signing our new CS engagement letter, calling it "an onerous contract of adhesion." Ultimately, though, he told me he thought he could live with it. As I recall, this was shortly after I told him that I thought CS could live without the Fairweather firm if it couldn't live with our engagement letter. I think Phil and I are starting to develop a nice understanding.

July 12, 1993. Phil invited me out for golf. I hardly know how to play, but I've decided to go out anyway. Of course, he'll beat me rather handily.

September 19, 1994. Life is beautiful here at CS. The public offering of CS stock was completed last week, and my shares are worth in the mid-seven figures. We now have four other attorneys in our legal department, including a former associate and a former partner from the Fairweather firm. While that's added well over a half million dollars to our expenses, we've saved more than three times that in reduced legal fees. Of course, Phil liked the good old days a lot better, but he's adjusting nicely to our new arrangement. I don't think he blew that 3-foot putt on the last hole intentionally last week so that I won fifty bucks from him, but who can say for sure?

Pressing for Information

I'M A REPORTER. In my job, I deal with lots of people. Of them all, the funniest are lawyers.

That may strike you as strange. Lawyers aren't necessarily known as stitches. And they don't mean to be. But they are. For all their supposed sophistication and verbal ability, most of them haven't the foggiest notion how to deal with the press. Let me give you an example of a recent series of articles I wrote about a law firm.

A couple months ago, I got a tip about some goings on at a large law firm, Fairweather, Winters & Sommers. According to my source, one of the members of the Fairweather executive committee, Stephen Falderall, was caught with his hand in the till. It seemed that he had been bilking both the firm and clients out of substantial sums of money.

I started my investigation by going to the person who I knew would know all of the details, Mr. Falderall's secretary. I sensed that she was not going to be cooperative when she denied that she knew Mr. Falderall. She referred me to the firm's public relations spokesperson, Nails Nuttree, the head of the firm's litigation section.

After I introduced myself as Marcella Robespierre, a reporter from *International Lawyer*, Mr. Nuttree said, "Ms. Robespierre, the Fairweather firm denies that Mr. Stephen Falderall embezzled more than a million dollars from clients and the firm or, in the alternative, denies that it had any prior knowledge of that wrongdoing and condemns it." Nails thanked me for giving him this opportunity to clarify the record and added that he was quite busy and so, regrettably, would not be able to talk to me further right now.

I pointed out to Mr. Nuttree that I had not yet told him the nature of what I was calling about, that for all he knew I might be calling to discuss the big case he had just won. Nails asked how I knew that he had just won a big case. I told him that I knew he was a litigator, and I had yet to call a litigator about anything who did not want to talk about the big case he had just won. (In fact, I have never met a litigator who lost a case, ever.)

"As a matter of fact, Marcie, I did just win a major victory," Nails allowed, "and I thought it a bit strange that the press had not picked up on it yet." He congratulated me on having uncovered his victory, but told me that he was not surprised, since *International Lawyer* was always on top of the news that mattered to the legal profession, unlike some of the scandal sheets that seemed only to be interested in the dirt in the profession. He told me that his name was spelled with two t's and two e's, but only one n, u and r. "Nails" was just like "hammer and nails" without the "hammer and," he joked. He said he might have a photo or two of himself around, if that would help me out any.

I told Nails that I didn't want to disturb him because he'd said he was quite busy. "Oh, pshaw, that's nonsense, Marcie, I'm never too busy to talk to a member of the working press," Nails said. But when I suggested that we start by talking about Mr. Falderall, Nails told me that he had a meeting he'd forgotten about that he needed to run out to right away.

So I ran my initial story about Falderall, which included the following:

Scandal has reached the inner sanctums of one of Chicago's most prestigious law firms, Fairweather, Winters & Sommers. For days, rumors have circulated about the billing practices of a member of the firm's executive committee, Stephen Falderall. Sources close to the matter confirmed to International Lawyer that Falderall is suspected of duping both the firm and its clients of over one million dollars through a scheme involving duplicate charges for photocopying. Firm spokesperson, Nails Nutree, said, "The Fairweather firm denies that Mr. Stephen Falderall embezzled more than a million dollars from clients and the firm or, in the alternative, denies that it had any prior knowledge of that wrongdoing and condemns it." The state disciplinary commission for lawyers is reportedly investigating the matter.

Immediately after the story appeared, I received an irate call from Nails complaining that I had misspelled his name in the article, leaving out a "t." I told him that the error was intentional, since I made it a practice of spelling correctly only the names of people who cooperate with me. Nails said that that was the lowest trick he'd ever heard of and threatened to make a call to my editor. I told him that he should feel free to do that, but that he shouldn't expect to see a mention of his recent trial victory if he did. Nails said that that sounded like blackmail to him and he wasn't going to be intimidated by any two-bit reporter into talking to her about something he didn't want to talk about. He said, though, that he did happen to have a little time this afternoon, and might squeeze me in, if I'd like to drop by his office.

When I came up to the thirty-second floor, the receptionist called Nails, and I was escorted into his corner office by his secretary, Florence. Nails asked if I would like some coffee or a soft drink, and when I said that a Coke would be nice, he asked if I had any change, since he was out. I fished through my purse for three quarters, handed them to Florence, then found another three when Nails said he'd love a root beer and promised to pay me back.

I took out my notebook and began to question Nails about the Falderall matter. Before we got started, Nails said, he wanted my agreement that prior to printing anything, I would submit it to him for his approval. I told him that that would be impossible, we would never consent to somebody approving a story. He said that he just wanted to check it for the grammar, that as a former English major it bothered him to appear in a story that was not grammatically correct. I told him that we had editors who specialized in grammar, and so he needn't worry.

In that case, Nails told me that he wanted this interview to be off the record. I protested that as spokesperson for the firm, he ought to be willing to comment for the record. Nails said that the Falderall case was too much of a hot potato, and that he would only talk to me if it were off the record. I pointed out to him that if it were off the record, I would not be able to put his name in the article and that therefore all of his concern about the spelling of his name would be moot. Nails said that that was okay, that he'd like to be referred to as "a highly placed source in a position to know." He said he'd always dreamt of being referred to in that way, because it sounded so "cloak-and-daggerish."

I told him that if he was to be referred to, the interview would not be off the record, but, instead, he would be speaking "not for attribution." He said that was fine with him, that all his life he'd spoken for attribution, and he'd like to try not.

I argued that if I spoke of "a highly placed person in a position to know," that everyone would know it was he who had spoken to me and that therefore he might just as

well go on the record. Nails admitted that there would be those who would suspect it was him, but that if he were not named, he could maintain plausible deniability, a posture he'd always wanted to be able to maintain. In the end, I agreed that his remarks would be "not for attribution." What follows is a portion of the article I wrote after my interview with Nails:

> The details of how Fairweather, Winters & Sommers executive committee member Stephen Falderall could have gotten away with billing over a million dollars of fraudulent photocopy charges to his clients are starting to come to light. A highly placed person in a position to know explained that Stephen was known around the firm as the "mad Xeroxer. Heck, you couldn't hardly put something down in Steve's presence without him picking it up, running down to the photocopy center and orderin' a hundred copies."
>
> It was Stephen's copying proclivity, explained this highly placed person in a position to know, that accounted for the fact that over the past seven years the Fairweather copy department contributed 17% of the firm's revenues and more than 22% of its net profits.
>
> Firm spokesperson Nails Nuttree, who recently won a major litigation case for an important client, said, "The Fairweather firm denies that Mr. Stephen Falderall embezzled more than a million dollars from clients and the firm or, in the alternative, denies that it had any prior knowledge of that wrongdoing and condemns it."

Mr. Nuttree's reaction to the article was mixed. He was pleased that I had spelled his name correctly, and delighted that I mentioned the case he'd won for a client. He was also pleased to see his photograph in *International Lawyer*. He says that he would have preferred that the caption to his photo read, "Chair of the Fairweather Litigation Department" rather than, "Highly Placed Person in a Position to Know."

Trial, By Juror

WHAT A DAY I HAD the other day, I'll tell ya. A thrill it was for me. I served my country. Me, Sylvia Shultz. Duty called. Sylvia served.

Maybe you're wondering, did we go to war or something, and you missed it? Relax. No, I was called to jury duty. Summoned, actually. I got a summons. It looked so official, it scared the heck out of me. Something about buying presents or something I didn't understand until I went next door and my neighbor, Harriet, explained it all to me.

How did they select me, Sylvia Shultz? I wondered. I mean, from all the many very qualified people to serve, they picked me. Naturally, I was honored. I mean I had no training, to speak of. Of course, I do have some experience. I watch Judge Wapner on *People's Court* and I used to watch *LA Law* religiously until it went under, and I watch Court TV every once in a while, especially when O.J. is on. So I'm not a total stranger to the law, if you know what I mean.

Still, I have to say, I was a little nervous. I mean, what do you wear? How do you act? Do I call the judge "judge" or "your honor" or "your worship" (like they do in those old British movies that I love, with the wigs and everything)? Naturally, I wanted to find out these things, so I shouldn't say the wrong thing and be held in contempt—though I don't exactly know what that means—and thrown into the clinker with hardened criminals and everything, and the food isn't good and they can put you at hard labor, which at my age and weight (which I'm not going to tell you, because it's none of your business) would not be a good thing for me.

Luckily, I had a couple weeks before my jury date, so I could bone up some. I read everything I could get my hands on to prepare. I started with the basics, the US Constitution, *Presumed Innocent*, the driver's license exam booklet . . . you know, the nitty and the gritty. Then I got into some more sophisticated stuff, *The Trial, Crime and Punishment, On Liberty*. I rented some old movies, and made an appointment to see my lawyer at Fairweather, Winters & Sommers, Harold Ratchet, to give me a few hints.

Mr. Ratchet was a bit confused. I came in and told him I had a few questions for him about jury duty. He said he didn't think he could help, I would have to serve. I said of course I would serve, I just wanted to know how I could be the best juror in the box.

Harold told me that I was the first client he'd ever heard from who *wanted* to serve on a jury. Most people called him wanting to figure out some way to get out of serving. That surprised me quite a bit.

Actually, Harold was not a whole lot of help, to be honest. You see he had never served, since lawyers are not asked to serve, I guess because they understand what is going on and, as I was to learn, they don't want anyone on the jury who understands what's going on. Also, since Harold was not a trial lawyer, he did not know what actually went on in court (which I guess should really have qualified him to serve on the jury, after all), but he suggested that I might want to watch Court TV or Judge Wapner.

So, anyway, the big day came, and I was so excited I could hardly sleep the night before. I was supposed to be at the courthouse by 8:30, but I was there before 8:00, which was a pretty good thing because it wasn't that easy to find the place where jurors were supposed to go. When I did, though, it was very nice because they had free coffee and donuts and a lady with a uniform sent me over to a desk to sign my name and to get a number, like in a bakery. There was a great big flag of the United States with a gold eagle on the top, and framed pictures of the governor and the mayor and a bunch of other muckety-mucks all around the room.

About 8:30, the lady with the uniform called for us all to quiet down and she began speaking. She thanked us all for coming and told us that what we were doing was essential to freedom and democracy and justice and several other very worthwhile causes. She then showed us a slideshow about the history of the jury system, which started in England and came over in the big revolution that happened a couple hundred years ago because of the Boston Tea Party, I think.

She told us that we should wait in this big room and that they would call people as they needed them, and that some of us might not be called at all. At that point, a lot of people pulled out books or newspapers or stuff that they'd brought along to work on. I did not bring anything along, so I decided to talk to the other people in the room and to take a little survey of my own as to how people felt about jury duty. Here's what I found:

- Joe Palkino thinks that jury duty should be given to the homeless, since it would be a way for them to earn some money
- Margaret Rhodes thinks that juries should either be all male or all female, since if they should wind up getting sequestered together there could be some wild sex parties
- Sarah Stroble thinks that people in the jury waiting room should be allowed to read in peace and

should not be bothered by other people in the jury waiting room
- Fred Brothelem thinks that there should be an odd number of jurors, so that there would always be somebody to break ties
- Anne Jackstraw thinks that nobody should be allowed on a jury who is unable to recite the Pledge of Allegiance by heart, unless they have a religious objection to it or a learning disability
- Bob Jackson looked over the comments I'd gotten so far and said that I could put him down for serving with Margaret Rhodes, if they get sequestered

It's not too scientific, the survey, but I'm sure it proves something. Anyway, just as my survey was picking up steam, the lady with the uniform announced that they needed a panel of jurors in courtroom 6, and asked that people with numbers 12 through 40 please line up and walk quietly down the corridor to the courtroom. Well, you probably can imagine my excitement when I realized that, as number 23 (the same number, coincidentally I'm sure, that Michael Jordan used to wear), I was well within those called.

The Judge in courtroom 6, Francine Standish, a lady, greeted us and told us that we would each be asked some questions by lawyers for both sides and, maybe, by her, too. She explained that this was a case involving a rather gory hit-and-run automobile accident and that there would likely be some fairly bloody physical evidence, so that anyone who felt he or she could not deal with that should say so now, and they would be excused.

Now, yours truly, me, Sylvia, was a little nervous about this. I don't do that well with mangled body parts. But I decided, what the heck, I had come this far and I wasn't going to back out now. Worst that could happen would be I'd whoops on a few of my fellow jurors. One juror lady did raise her hand, though, and was dismissed. The judge thanked her, though I have no idea why, since she hadn't done anything but drop out.

At this point, they started questioning the jurors, one by one. Some of them were excused and others were accepted. I was getting nervous when finally they got to me. The answers below come directly from the lady who took them down with that funny little machine that makes marks that nobody can understand (she sent this to me because I said I wanted it for my scrapbook). I've made a few little comments in brackets.

> Mr. Conway [a really sharp dresser, 3-piece suit, gold cuff links]: Mrs. Shultz?
> Mrs. Shultz: Yes. [This first question was easy and, therefore, a terrific confidence-builder for me.]
> Mr. Conway: I'd like to ask you a few questions about your driving, Mrs. Shultz.
> Mrs. Shultz: Go right ahead.
> Mr. Conway: Have you ever had a traffic accident?
> Mrs. Shultz: No, but I've caused a lot of them. [I drive very slow and get people around me pretty nervous, so they do some foolish things.]
> Mr. Conway: I see. Well, my client is accused of hitting a pedestrian and leaving the scene of the crime. Do you think that you could give him a fair trial, judge the evidence impartially?
> Mrs. Shultz: Oh, absolutely. Neither a borrower nor a lender be, I always say.
> Mr. Conway: You do? What do you mean by that?
> Mrs. Shultz: I'm not too sure, but it does have a certain even-handedness to it, don't you think?
> Mr. Conway: Yes, definitely. Mr. Whelan?
> Mr. Whelan [short and frumpy, like my ex-husband]: Mrs. Shultz.
> Mrs. Shultz: Still me.
> Mr. Whelan: That's good. I represent the State, Mrs. Shultz.

Mrs. Shultz: The whole state. My goodness, what a guy you must be, Mr. Whelan.

Mr. Whelan: No, what's meant by that is the State in a criminal case brings the charges, and is entitled to a fair trial just the way the defendant is, Mrs. Shultz.

Mrs. Shultz: Nothing else would be fair, would it?

Mr. Whelan: Absolutely not. And if you were to become a juror, you would do your best to give both sides a fair shake?

Mrs. Shultz: More than fair.

Mr. Whelan: What do you mean "more than fair," Mrs. Shultz?

Mrs. Shultz: I mean, I would bend over backwards to both sides, which would mean that I would be straight up, fair as a judge, no offense, Your Honor.

Judge: No offense, Mrs. Shultz.

So, that was the end of my questioning. They went on to question numbers 24 through 37, until they wound up with a full panel, including me. By now, it was about four o'clock, so the judge told us we were dismissed for the rest of the day, but should report back directly to courtroom 6 at 9:00 the next morning.

Next day I get back to the courthouse early and go into the juror waiting room to say hello to some of my old friends from yesterday. I get in there and I see the lady with the uniform, but none of my friends from yesterday. I ask the lady about that and she tells me that there'll be a whole new group today. I tell her that I was selected for a jury in courtroom 6. She congratulates me, and tells me to do my best.

I get down to courtroom 6, and the judge isn't there yet. Pretty soon, a guy comes in and says something like, "All rise, this honorable court and all the accoutrements and appurtenances and so forth, the honorable judge presiding, is in session, God save the Queen." (Actually, I made up the "God save the Queen," from the old British movies.)

So we all rise, and the judge comes in, and we all sit. And the judge says to us, "ladies and gentlemen of the jury, after you went home last evening, counsel met and have reached a settlement of this case. Therefore, we will not need your services today. On behalf of the state and myself, I want to thank you for your willingness to serve in this case. You are now dismissed and may go to the jury waiting room to collect your check."

I got paid for two days' service, plus car fare, $34.74 in all. I didn't cash it. I've got it framed in the den, with pictures I got of Mr. Conway, Mr. Whelan and Judge Standish, all signed "To Sylvia, A great juror."

So that's justice. They also serve who only stand and wait.

Lawyer:English Dictionary

SEARCHING FOR PROJECTS that would serve to improve the understanding between themselves and the lawyers who represent them, the Fairweather Clients Association hit upon the idea of creating a dictionary to translate what lawyers say into language that a layperson might understand. Below are selections from the first edition of that dictionary, which hit the bookstores weeks ago—and has yet to sell a copy.

Introduction

Most lawyers once spoke English, some of them fluently. Then they went to law school and learned how to write and talk like lawyers. This disability has been aggravated by years of practice with their seniors, who have painstakingly excised any vestiges of simple, straightforward language that may have survived in young associates.

The result is that lawyers have difficulty communicating with clients, and vice versa. Clients generally have no idea what their lawyers are saying to them. Worse, some clients think they understand.

This dictionary is meant to help you communicate with your lawyer. We recommend that you keep one copy of the dictionary in your office, one in the car, and one on-hand at home. When your lawyer speaks, don't be afraid to stop him in mid-sentence and consult your dictionary. Remember that it's not just fancy Latin phrases you need to look up in this dictionary. When lawyers use ordinary words, they ordinarily don't have the ordinary meaning you associate with them. In fact, talking to a lawyer is a little bit like going to England and discovering that "boot" means the trunk of your car.

Since lawyers are constantly thinking of new ways to confuse clients, we anticipate having to publish a new edition of the *Unabridged Lawyer:English Dictionary* approximately every six weeks. In order to keep our editors current on the latest lawyerese, we request that you, our readers, send in any new phrases your lawyer may have conjured up, together with your best stab at what those phrases may mean.

Definitions

contingent fee a fee arrangement negotiated by an attorney in a case the attorney feels is a sure winner, thus eliminating any contingency other than the amount of the fee

business risk the term applied by an attorney to describe any risk involved in any potential action or inaction, thereby transferring complete responsibility for any possible failure from the attorney to the client

I haven't heard from the other side (generally used in response to a client's question as to the status of a matter) means that the attorney has forgotten to call the other side, as he had promised to do the week before last

Witnesseth means absolutely nothing

mens rea is the opposite of women's rea

in the range of $25,000 to $30,000 (typically used in estimating a legal fee) means the fee will be a minimum of $30,000-$40,000, and probably considerably higher

around $300,000 (used in describing average partner income in the firm last year to a legal reporter) means between $150,000 and $160,000

how're things going (spoken by a lawyer to a potential client) means do you have any major piece of legal work that I could do for you at a premium fee, please

corporate seal a cast metal die used to emboss a circle with illegible writing onto documents so as to give the corporate secretary a purpose in life; also, the mascot of certain marine companies

Friday (in response to a question as to when a particular matter will be handled by your lawyer) means a week from next Tuesday, at the earliest

just calling to see how you are (spoken by a lawyer to a potential client) means do you have any major piece of legal work that I could do for you at a premium fee, please

including, without limiting the generality of the foregoing means these are all the things we could think of, but—believe it or not—there may be even more

say hello to your lovely wife means the lawyer has no idea what your spouse's name is, but has managed to recall her gender

deposition a meeting in which a lawyer from one side of the case gets to ask a witness from another side of the case all about what he's going to testify to in court so that when he does testify, that lawyer can trip him up by pointing out minute and inconsequential differences between what he said in the deposition and what he said in court.

hi means your first billable hour has just commenced

brief a very long document in which each side sets out, *ad nauseam*, all of the arguments as to why it should win the case

ad nauseam the manner in which each side sets out in a brief all of the arguments as to why it should win the case

boiler plate standard language, generally of little or no import, that is inserted into a contract or other document in order to make the document longer and thereby justify a larger fee for the lawyer preparing the document; also, a metal element attached to the front of a boiler

hello (spoken by a lawyer to a potential client) means do you have any major piece of legal work that I could do for you at a premium fee, please

may it please the court (used to begin oral argument in a case) is an alternative to a lawyer clearing his throat

absolutely not, under no circumstances (used by a lawyer in a negotiation) means my client and I would prefer not to give this point away just yet, if you don't mind

ad damnum the amount sought in a case, which typically represents the largest number the complaining attorney can think of, and need bear no relationship to the amount in controversy

why don't you let me get that (said by a lawyer when reaching for a restaurant check) means you can either pay for it now, or it will show up on your bill with the firm's normal 25% mark-up

intentional tort a wrong done by one party to another that is not a negligent tort; for example, a fellow arguing with another person over a parking space who walks over and rips the person's nose off

negligent tort a wrong done by one party to the other that is not an intentional tort; for example, a doctor performing plastic surgery involving a tummy tuck who accidentally rips the patient's nose off

Dr. Frederick Tucker's spouse, Mary Louise Tucker, hereinafter sometimes referred to as 'Mary' (when preceded by "this is") indicates a lawyer introducing Fred Tucker's wife, Mary, to somebody at a cocktail party

in the alternative inconsistent arguments which signal that the lawyer making them has no idea where his client's case's strength lies, but hopes fervently that the court will discover it somewhere for him

may I borrow your pen means may I have your pen

litigator (in a large law firm) means an attorney who watched Perry Mason as a kid, excelled at debate in high school and college, was a member of the winning moot court team in law school, knows how to prepare and answer interrogatories, take depositions, argue motions, and settle cases, and hopes to actually try a case sometime before he dies or retires

my partner Harry is an expert in ___ law means Harry has heard of the area of law and can converse about it convincingly for five minutes at a cocktail party

res judicata Latin term meaning we've decided that matter already, you big dummy

retirement (when applied to a significant partner in a large law firm) death

can I get back to you on that means that the lawyer does not have the foggiest idea what to say next, but may be able to come up with a response in a week or two

legal malpractice a lawyer who does something so incredibly stupid that even another lawyer feels comfortable testifying against him

let's do lunch sometime (spoken to anybody other than a client or potential client) means "let's not do lunch, ever"

one-quarter hour (on a time sheet) five minutes; (as a statement of when the lawyer will be available to see the client) forty minutes

[EDITOR'S NOTE: the redactors of the *Unabridged Lawyer:English Dictionary* considered presenting the definitions in alphabetical order, but concluded that since most of the meanings were arbitrary, so too should be the order of their presentation.]

Setting the Ground Rules

THE SUBCOMMITTEE of the fledgling Fairweather Clients Association, which was founded to study the shape that the new client organization should take, was composed of Rebecca Fissure, Sheik Hamurabi etc. (Ben-Ben) and Leonard Jenkins. At Ben-Ben's insistence, they met in secret, at a time and place known only to them. Rebecca called the meeting to order and asked Ben-Ben if he would mind taking minutes.

"We are going to have a written record of this?" asked Ben-Ben.

"Of course we are," answered Rebecca. "We have to report to the group on what we did."

"But to report in writing, I don't know. . ."

"Why do you have this compulsion about secrecy, Ben-Ben?" inquired Leonard. "I don't get it."

"Because a sheep in the wilderness. . ."

"Look, Ben-Ben, we've got to get beyond sheep, okay? Nobody cares that we are meeting and forming this group, so there's no need for extreme security measures."

"Then why are we meeting, if nobody cares?"

"*We* care. It's just that nobody else does; that's the nature of most committees, so you don't have to worry."

"Well, okay, if you're sure."

"We're sure," said Rebecca and Leonard, in unison.

"Fine, then I'll take notes. What am I supposed to write down?"

"The important decisions we make."

"We are empowered to make important decisions, just the three of us?"

"Actually, no. But we will make recommendations."

"So then it's the important recommendations I should write down?"

"Yes."

"But how will I know what's important?"

"Whatever you write down will be important."

"And whatever I don't, won't?"

"Exactly."

"I think I am going to like this position."

"Good, now let's get to the name of our organization first."

"Wasn't Byron Fair going to ask his uncle, Stanley Fairweather, about whether we could use the name Fairweather Clients Association?" asked Leonard.

"Yes, and he did."

"And what did Stanley say?"

"He said that legally we'd have a problem doing that, since nobody in our group is named Fairweather."

"So then we can't use it?"

"No, we can."

"I don't understand," said Ben-Ben. "I thought there's a legal problem in using it."

"There is. But Stanley pointed out that our group was going to be composed of many—perhaps, eventually, most—of the firm's clients. He thought it was highly unlikely that the firm would choose to bring a lawsuit against most of its clients because they used part of the firm name."

"Great, so that settles the name. What's next?"

"We need to decide on the purpose of the association."

"Well, I'd say getting together for drinks, and meals or snacks," offered Leonard.

"I don't see us primarily as a drinking and eating society," said Rebecca. "That's incidental to our purposes."

"Incidental to some may prove central to others," observed Leonard.

"Well said," commented Ben-Ben.

"Thanks."

"I thought that the physical therapy was extremely useful, and I'd like to keep that as a part of our purpose," added Ben-Ben.

"Well, to me the focus ought to be on what we can learn from one another, as clients, and how we can together work to form a more effective relationship with the Fairweather firm, so as to get better service as clients, improve the quality of the legal product and stem the ever-rising tide of legal costs in our society," suggested Rebecca.

"Ben-Ben, you're crying," noticed Leonard.

"That's the most beautiful thing I've ever heard in my life . . . 'stem the ever-rising tide,' it's poetry. You're the Lord Byron of purpose clause writers, Rebecca."

"Thanks a lot, Ben-Ben. I'm glad you're so moved."

"Shouldn't this group give us some economic muscle, allow us to get a better deal on our fees?" asked Leonard.

"Why are you interested in fees? I thought you were a pro bono client."

"Sure, now I'm pro bono, but I don't plan to be pro bono forever. And when I'm not, I don't want to have to pay the outrageous fees you people are swallowing."

"Why do we have to pick and choose between purposes? Can't we slop a bunch of them into a purpose clause and be done with it?" asked Rebecca.

"Yes, I suppose we could do that. Who do you think should be eligible to be members?"

"I would think that as the Fairweather Clients Association, the answer to that would be rather obvious," suggested Leonard.

"Well, of course, it will be clients. But what is a client?"

"What do you mean, 'what is a client?' You sound like Ben-Ben and his sheep. A client is somebody who pays fees for legal services and. . ."

"That would exclude you, Leonard, since you don't pay fees. And, as I recall when I was at the firm, there were quite a few others who didn't pay their fees, who were not pro bono. I don't think we want to get into examining the firm's books to see who is an eligible member."

"No, you're right."

"And at a corporation, who is the client? The president, the general counsel, members of the board of directors, employees? And what about clients who cease to become clients because they go out of business, or merge? Do they get booted out of the FCA unceremoniously just because of that?

"I guess it's not so easy, after all. Maybe we should throw membership open to everyone," suggested Leonard.

"You mean just let anyone join?"

"I suppose that would be the implication of throwing membership open to everyone, Ben-Ben."

"Well, I'm against that."

"Why are you against it?"

"If I'm going to be a member of some secret organization, I don't want it to be open to every Tom, Dick and Jerry."

"You mean Harry."

"What?"

"It's every Tom, Dick and Harry, not Jerry."

"I thought it's open to everyone."

"It is."

"Well, then Jerry can join, too. I mean I certainly don't see any point in opening the group up to everyone except people named Jerry, do you?"

"No, I guess not, Ben-Ben."

"Opening it to everyone does have certain advantages," suggested Rebecca.

"For instance?"

"Well, we should be able to keep dues down if we have a large membership."

"You mean there are going to be dues?" asked Leonard. "Even for pro bono clients?"

"We might have a sliding scale, I suppose. And if we had a large number of members, we might be able to provide services, like health insurance benefits, discounts on automobile rentals, travel services. . ."

"This is starting to sound better," said Ben-Ben. "Maybe we could develop our own credit card, too. I'm definitely going to put this into the minutes."

"You mean that's the first thing you've written down"?

"It's the first thing that's important."

"What about the name, and the purpose?"

"Those weren't important."

"How do you know they weren't important?"

"Because I didn't write them down, and what I don't write down isn't important.

"Ben-Ben, you blockhead."

"It's okay, Leonard; I remember what we discussed so far. And, before we adjourn, we should talk about voting rights," said Rebecca.

"What about them?" asked Leonard.

"Would each member get one vote, or would each client be entitled to only one vote?"

"I say one man, one vote," said Leonard.

"Maybe votes should be allocated to clients according to their billings from the Fairweather firm," suggested Ben-Ben.

"Sorta cuts me out, doesn't it," observed Leonard.

"And I thought we were going to open the association up to non-clients," said Rebecca.

"Just because we open membership up to everyone doesn't mean everyone gets a vote," Ben-Ben pointed out.

"No, I guess that's right. Listen, I think we've made pretty good progress today. Maybe it's time to turn this over to counsel to draft some articles of association," suggested Rebecca. "I thought I'd call somebody over at the Fairweather firm to help out."

"Won't that be expensive?" asked Ben-Ben.

"Heck no. In fact, I think I can get them to take this on on a pro bono basis," offered Leonard.

"How are you going to do that?" asked Ben-Ben.

"By asking them how they'd feel about one of their prime law firm competitors representing the Fairweather Clients Association."

Talking About the Law

I TAME DE LIONS, dat's vat I do. Yah, in de cages I tame dem, de lions. Und ve perform, in de circus.

Dat's a dancherous job, vat I do, yah? But I luff it. Since I vas a tiny tike I vant to do dis, tame de lions.

You notice maybe I shpeak mit an accent. I come from Chermany, dat's vere I vas born und I lived dere until I vas thirty-vun years of age. Den I come ofer to dis country und I shtay here now twenty-four years. I like it here very much. It's a vunderful country you haf, a gute life you live here.

You like to know sometink about my verk, I tink, yah? Vell, I tell you. I shtart ven I'm six to learn to tame de lions. My fahter teach me. He's lion tamer, too. Und his fahter, too. Und his fahter, too. But, mit me, de lion tamers in my family come to an end. Hans, my boy, vill not be lion tamer. No.

Anyvay, ven I'm askink to learn de lion taming, my fahter say to me, "Helga, you must. . ."

Yes, I am a voman. You are surprised? Vy?

He say to me, "Helga, you must alvays remember vun tink if you vant to be a lion tamer."

"Vat is dat tink, Papa?" I ask him.

"Du solst die ketzen nicht aufgepissen," he answered. This means you should never piss off de cats. I'm sorry to use dat verd, but dat's vat my fahter tell me. Und it's very gute advice.

My fahter learn dis advice from his fahter. Und he learned it from his fahter ven a lion kill him. Ven you see dis lesson, you vill remember it, dat's for sure.

You see, my fahter explain to me, de lions are much shtronger den ve are. If dey vant to, dey can tear us apart. De job of de lion tamer, my fahter tell me, is to make de lion not vant to tear him apart.

Dis he must do in different vays. First, de tamer must make de lion to fear him. To do dis, he must hurt de lion a little bit ven de lion is young, because dis is de only way you can teach a lion. Mit de lion, you cannot reason. Und, after, ven de lion get older, you must remind de lion, from time to time, dat you are able to hurt him, because othervise he forgets. Dis is vy ve use de vip und shnap it in front of de lion, to remind him.

Second, you must be de friend of de lion. You may tink dat dis is not possible ven you also vant de lion to fear you, but it is possible. Ven you are not hurting de lion, you are very kind to de lion. You pet de lion, you feed de lion, you talk nice to de lion, you give de lion vater. Ven you are kind to de lion, de lion vants to be kind to you, also.

Third, you must let de lion know who you are. Because, if you vant de lion to fear you und to be your friend, den he must know you. Dis means each day you vear the same clothes, you valk und talk the same vay, you do not vear perfumes.

Fourth, you never show any fear of de lion, by backink avay or duckink or anytink else. Dis you must practice outside de cage, mit people jumping out at you, so ven the lion moves qvickly, you vill not be schkared. You alvays look right at de lions und never turn your back on dem.

Fifth, you must not let de lion know how powerful he is. Dis means dat even ven he is not threatening you, you must control vat he does. If he begins to tear tinks, you

must shtop him the same vay you vould shtop him if he vas tearing you, because if he gets de idea dat he can tear up utter tinks, he may get de idea he can tear up you, too.

But you must not control de lion completely. For example, he vill growl und throw his head around, vich natchurally is an aggressive act. But you vant him to growl und throw his head. Vy? Because in de circus show, you vant de audience to hear him growl so dey vill see how dancherous he is to you und how brave you are to be in de cage mit him. So ven de lion growls ven you are alone mit him, you revard him in de same vey you do ven he does sometink you vant him to do, like shtandink on a shtool.

Sixth, du solst die ketzen nicht aufgepissen. I know dat you undershtand dis bit of Cherman. De reason for dis is because, though you have trained de lion to fear you und to like you, de lion is shtill de lion, und he forgets everytink vat you teach him very qvickly ven he becomes angry or confused. De lion does not like shurprises, so if you are shmart, you vill be very, very careful not to shurprise him.

You may be tinkink dat de performance vill shurprise de lion, mit all de noise und de people. But no, he is not shurprised by dese tinks. De lights shine on de cage und de rest of de tent is dark, so he does not see de people. Und de noise is no shurprise, because vhen ve train de lions, ve play records of de crowd noise, so de lions get used to it.

So deese are de rules I follow. Of course, dis does not mean dat de job is not dancherous. Some lions ve get who ve cannot train, dey belong in de jungle, or at least in de zoo. Ve try to find dose out ven dey are very young. In dis vay ve do not vaste a lot of time trying to train dem. In dis vay also ve do not find out at a time ven dey are so big dat dey can easily und qvickly cause serious dancher.

Und in dis vay ve find dem at a time ven dey do not teach de utter lions dere bad habits.

So you are ready now to be a lion tamer, yah? I tink probably no, yah? Because dere is a big difference betveen undershtanding vat's involved und deciding to put your head in de lion's mouth. Even if de lion is perfectly trained, you better hope dat he doesn't have to shneeze at dat moment. Because, if he does, somebody else is going to have to say, "Gesundheit."

But vat does all of dis have to do mit de lawyers, you are vonderink. I could tell you how de rules dat I gave you for taming de lions apply also in de law, de vays in vhich de lawyer is like de lion tamer. Ve might even say dat de lion is like de client. Ve could talk about how de lawyer uses his power und fear und frendliness in de same vay like de lion tamer. Or ve could substitute for "die ketzen" in Papa's rule, "der judch" or "der client."

Yes, ve could do all of dis. Und perhaps, it vould be interestink to some people. Dis is vat you lawyers do all de time. You play mit verds und concepts. But dat is not vy I told you all about lion taming ven I vas asked to talk about de lion tamer's view of de lawyer. No.

I have met in dis country a lot of lawyers. Dis is because my son, Hans, he is a young lawyer mit de firm of Fairvetter, Vinter und Zohmer. Und venever ve get togetter mit lawyers, Hans und me, de only tink dey vant to talk about is de law, und dere cases und utter lawyers. Ven ve lion tamers leave de cage, de last tink ve vant to talk about is de lion. But dese lawyers, dey never leave de cage, dey never leave dere verk behind dem. Und, verse, dey tink dat everybody is so faschinated mit dem und mit de law. Vell, dey are wrong. Ve are not faschinated by de law. Ve are bored silly by de law.

Und so, dat's vat I vant to say to lawyers. Perhaps you vere interested to hear about de lion tamink. If dat is de case, you might be interested in vat utter people have to say, too, if you vould take de time to ask dem, und to listen.

Or perhaps you vere not so interested by de lion tamink. Dat's okay, too. But, in dat case, remember dat you are hearink only vunce about de lion tamink. Just try to imagine how all of us lion tamers, und doctors, und business people, und artists, und teachers, und social vorkers, und everybody else feels about hearink about your cases over und over, every time ve see you.

Und so, as my new teenage lion tamer apprentice (who, by de vay, is de son of a lawyer) vould say, "C'mon you lawyers, get a life."

Total Quality Overmanagement

FAIRWEATHER CLIENTS ASSOCIATION member Jack Rite wrote the following letter to Stanley Fairweather regarding the firm's new total quality management program.

Dear Stanley:

I thought you would be interested in hearing about my recent experience with your TQM program.

Just a couple months ago, I called Sherman Clayton, the partner in charge of revising the draft of our agreement with Toledo Sheet & Tube for us, to ask when he thought we might have copies of the revised draft. He said he'd check on it and get right back to me. Two hours later he called and provided me with a detailed status report.

Immediately after my call, Sherman told me, he walked down to the photocopy center to see where my documents stood. He discovered that they were third in line, behind copying jobs being done for clients of his partners, Nails Nuttree and Alphonse Proust.

So Sherman walked down three flights to Nails' office and waited there twenty-five minutes while Nails finished a conversation with a client who was suing an insurance company for failure to pay on their flood insurance because they claimed that Nails' client was negligent in leaving several valuable items on the floor, where they would be damaged by any seepage into the basement. When Nails finally got off the phone, Sherman asked him if his copying job could wait until after mine, since I had called Sherman to inquire as to when my agreement would be delivered. At first, Sherman told me, Nails was reluctant to agree, but Sherman persuaded him by writing out and signing a note authorizing Nails to push his copy job ahead of any job that the photocopy department might be doing for Sherman at any time in the future.

Sherman then went to find Alphonse Proust to try to get him to agree to let Sherman put my copy job ahead of Alphonse's client. Unfortunately, Alphonse was not in the office at the time. Sherman ascertained from Alphonse's secretary, Fran, though, that Alphonse was out of town and would not be returning for a week and a half. Fran said that she had no instructions to send anything out in his absence, so that it would be safe to push Sherman's job ahead of Alphonse's.

Sherman then rushed back to the photocopy center to tell the operator the good news, only to find that the machine had broken down, and so they were unable to do anyone's job. The service company for the machine had assured the head of photocopy that they would send a serviceman out just as soon as they freed somebody up, but that that might be quite a while since they were very busy, because their machines broke down frequently. At that point, Sherman said, he determined to take things into his own hands and stripped to the waist and began to take the photocopy machine apart himself. Within ten minutes, Sherman had located the problem—one of the operators had accidentally hit the "off" button on the machine.

Sherman waited at the copy center until my job was completed, in order to assure that no other partner tried to bludgeon the head of photocopy into pushing his or her work ahead of mine. When the photocopying was completed, Sherman checked carefully to see that each document had all pages, then ran back to his secretary's station to make sure that she had typed the cover letter to me. Unfortunately, Sherman's secretary was on a cigarette break, which meant that she was unreachable, since, because the building is smoke-free, she had to go outside of the building in order to have a drag.

After searching through her desk, however, Sherman found the letter, ran down with the letter and agreements to the messenger department and instructed the messenger chief, Hurry Lopes, to pick the fastest and most trustworthy of his winged-footed messengers to deliver the envelope to me ASAP. Sherman then hustled back up to his office to call me and report (slightly winded) that the agreements would be over to my company in three shakes of a lamb's tail.

In days of yore, Sherman explained, he might have sent his secretary to track down where the agreements stood, but fortunately for us clients the Fairweather firm no longer has the wasteful practice of hiring a secretary for each lawyer. Now you operate on a 1:3 or 1:4 ratio of secretaries to lawyers. That saves us clients a lot of money, but of course it means that the secretaries have to be employed efficiently, doing what they do best, not running around the firm tracking down documents. Instead, partners can do that at $250/hour.

And, of course, Sherman pointed out, a lawyer can do that a lot more effectively than a secretary can. If Sherman's secretary had approached Nails about delaying his copy job so that Sherman's could be done promptly, Nails might have brushed her off. But when Sherman approached his partner directly, he accomplished the task, pronto.

Someone might question the need for Sherman to contact Alphonse, since Al was out of town. But, of course, one can always second guess. That's pretty easy, with

20/20 hindsight. The point is that Sherman took the initiative, went that extra step to get the job done for his client—and I, for one, appreciate that.

While the breakdown in photocopying was unfortunate, we clients understand that total quality management does not mean that nothing will ever go wrong. No firm can guarantee that. What it means is that the firm will do its best to avoid problems, but, when they occur, it will press into action to solve them, do whatever needs to be done, go the extra mile, make it right. And Sherman certainly did that.

Perhaps he didn't need to rip off his shirt to find out that the machine had not been turned on, but that's just more second guessing. Sherman sized up the situation in a split second—the machine was down. Having been trained in TQM, what ran through his mind was, "I've got to do whatever it takes to fix it. Sure I'm a lawyer. Sure I've never fixed anything in my life. Sure I don't have the foggiest idea what needs to be done. But I've got to get in there and get my hands dirty. Oops, hands dirty, these things can get messy. I'd better rip my shirt off." And so he did. Now it might have been a good idea to check to see whether the machine was on first, but in the heat of battle you don't always react rationally.

And it's not just that the firm got the job done. They didn't stop there. Heck no. They followed up.

First off, I got a lovely handwritten note from the photocopy operator apologizing for the delay caused by his accidentally turning the machine off, and pledging to do his utmost to avoid a recurrence of that. That was nice, but the firm didn't stop there, either.

No way. A few days later, I got a registered letter from the head of the photocopy department telling me that the offending photocopy operator, the nice fellow who wrote me the apologetic note, had been relieved of his duties. Now, at first that seemed a bit harsh, but on reflection I realized that when you're after total quality, you've got to send a clear message to your troops that sloppiness simply will not be tolerated.

And I'm happy to report that your firm did not rest there, either. Not at all. No more than a week later, I got a call from the head of the Total Quality Control Committee at the firm, asking if he could come over to talk to me to ascertain whether I was satisfied with the services I received on the matter. And then, a couple of weeks after that, I got a four-page survey from the firm's quality control consultants, Tellem, Whathey, Noh, soliciting my views on my recent experience.

Not long after the survey, Sherman called to invite me out to lunch. And what did Sherman want? He wanted to know whether I was satisfied with the quality of the meeting I had with the Total Quality Control Committee chair and whether the scope and content of the survey I was sent by the firm's consultants seemed appropriate.

In short, Stanley, I am overwhelmed by your concern for the quality of your interactions with me, your client. At the same time, I know that you appreciate that my time, like that of your partners, is valuable. Figuring my hourly rate at the same level as Sherman Clayton's, I have deducted the dollar value of my time consumed by your TQM efforts and enclose the balance due on your $40,000 statement—$85.22. Thanks for caring.

Sincerely,

Jack Rite

Legal Lemon Aid

ROBERTA HIRAM-BETTY, the daughter of Rodriguez Hiram-Betty, an attorney at the firm of Fairweather, Winters & Sommers, and Alice Hiram-Betty, a lawyer with the crosstown law firm of Phlatts and Sharps, wrote the following essay in her third-grade class on the assigned topic, "About My Mommy and Daddy."

My mommy and daddy are lawyers. Both of them are.

There are good things and bad things about having a mommy and daddy who are both lawyers. One of the good things is that I always have a lot of paper to write and draw on. But the bad thing is that the paper is all yellow with green lines on it.

I'm not exactly sure what my mommy and daddy do, but I think that they're spies. That's because everything is so secret. They each have a study and their doors are always locked. You need one of those key cards to get in, and they both have different cards. Once Mommy lost her purse, and she couldn't get into her office at home. Daddy broke in, but the alarm went off and the police came and arrested Daddy. They let him go in a few hours, though. Mommy represented him.

My brother, Edward, and I get along pretty good. He's in the fifth grade. When he and I have an argument, Mommy and Daddy each represent one of us. They change off, so we each have a chance to be represented by them. The only thing is that when they represent us, they deduct their fees from our allowances. I've talked to Mommy about representing me pro bono, but she says that she does enough for me pro bono as it is. They say that paying their fees is good for me and Edward, because it teaches us that there's a cost associated with dispute resolution. The other day, Edward wanted to appear pro se on an argument we had about some computer game we were playing, but Mommy and Daddy wouldn't let him do it.

Last summer, Edward and I got into some pretty heated negotiations over a lemonade stand that we wanted to set up. I wanted to just go ahead and do it, but Daddy said that that would be foolish. There were lots of issues that needed to be resolved. Such as what, I wanted to know.

Well, for starters Daddy pointed out that Edward and I would have to decide who would do what work at the stand. I thought I'd be good at making the lemonade and Edward could sell it. That was okay, but Daddy pointed out that there were a lot of other things that needed to be done. Somebody would have to move all of the stuff out to the corner, somebody would have to clean up, somebody would have to make the signs to advertise the stand, somebody would have to collect and keep track of the money, and somebody would have to provide the napkins and ice and straws, and would there be cookies, he wondered?

Of course, Mommy pointed out that there were financial considerations. How would Edward and I be paying for all of the supplies—the lemonade, the cups, the napkins, and materials for signs and leaflets, if we were going to use them? Money does not grow on trees, she is fond of pointing out, though I never recall saying I thought it did.

Daddy said he thought he and Mommy might be willing to invest in this start-up venture of ours, if the terms could be worked out satisfactorily. Daddy thought a convertible preferred of some sort would make sense, and suggested a coupon of 7 or 8% as appropriate. Edward asked if Daddy and Mommy, as potential investors, did not have something of a conflict of interest in advising us. Mommy thought Edward had a point and suggested that our neighbors, the Frances, who were both lawyers themselves, might be willing to serve as our counsel.

So we went over to the Frances', whose daughter, Enid, is a good friend of mine. We caught the Frances' in the midst of an argument over how late Enid could stay up that night. She was pushing for 9:00, because she *really* wanted to see a show called *The Killer Dragons Meet Godzilla's Aunt Ethel*. Enid promised that if she could stay up, just this once, she would always be good and would never ask for anything again for the rest of her life.

Mommy pointed out that Enid's promise probably would not be enforceable and, in any case, was inherently unbelievable. Enid told Mommy to butt out, that nobody had asked her opinion on the subject. Mr. Frances told Enid to mind her mouth.

Daddy, taking up Enid's case, suggested that perhaps her parents would be willing to tape the program and allow her to watch it at another time. Enid said that her parents were lawyers and so were incapable of operating the VCR. That meant she would either wind up getting another program taped or having the program cut off in the middle, which was worse than not seeing it at all.

Enid offered her parents five dollars to let her watch *The Killer Dragons Meet Godzilla's Aunt Ethel*. Mommy was shocked that Enid would offer her parents money to watch a TV show. Enid said that there was no reason to be shocked about that, hadn't Mommy heard of pay per view?

Mrs. Frances allowed that it was not so much the time that bothered her, but the choice of program. Enid took strong exception to her mother screening the programs she watched, calling it censorship of the worst type and questioning the constitutionality of the screening. Mommy doubted that there was a constitutional question, since the First Amendment applied only to the federal government and, through the Fourteenth Amendment, to the states. Neither Mr. nor Mrs. Frances was a state, Mommy pointed out. Perhaps not yet, Enid countered, but she happened to know that the Children's Legal Defense Fund was briefing the issue of whether a parent should be regarded as a state for purposes of the Constitution because of the authority they exert over children.

I reminded everyone that we had come over to the Frances' to seek counsel in the matter of our setting up a lemonade stand, and the possible financing of that venture by Mommy and Daddy. I asked whether the Frances would be available to represent me and Edward in the transaction. Enid said she thought that setting up a lemonade stand sounded like a neat idea, and asked whether she could help out. I thought that was a super idea, but Mommy pointed out that, if Enid participated, we would have to reach agreements with her and that, in that case, the Frances would be conflicted out of representing me and Edward.

So I told Enid that she couldn't be part of our lemonade operation, which started her to crying. The Frances were so upset to see their daughter in tears that they decided to allow her to stay up to see *The Killer Dragons Meet Godzilla's Aunt Ethel*, if she promised to stop crying, which she managed to do immediately.

Mr. Frances said that he would be happy to represent me, and that Mrs. Frances could represent Edward, but they would both, of course, need a retainer. We told the Frances that we didn't have the money right now, but could pay them out of our next allowances. Enid offered that, since she wasn't going to have to pay the five bucks to see her TV show, she would be happy to advance the retainer on our behalf, secured by a pledge of our next allowance payments. She suggested that we might want to talk to her parents about them reducing their legal fees and taking a part of the lemonade action instead. After discussion, the Frances agreed to take a fifteen percent equity interest in the lemonade stand in lieu of legal fees.

Just as we began to talk about the details of the lemonade business, the Frances' doorbell rang and in walked Jason and Pamela Lardner and their parents, Cynthia and Leroy, another lawyer couple who lived on the next block. It seems that Jason and Pamela, coincidentally, had also thought about setting up a lemonade business and had run into the same potential conflict with their parents, who were considering an investment. Mommy suggested that perhaps the Lardners should set up a stand on their block and that Edward and I could set up one on our block. Leroy Lardner, though, nixed that idea since he thought that their block was not as affluent as ours and therefore would not be as fertile territory for a lemonade business. He also thought that Mommy's suggestion that we carve up the lemonade market was blatantly an agreement in restraint of trade and hence invalid under the antitrust laws.

Ultimately, after several hours of negotiations, we reached agreement with the Frances and the Lardners on the structure of a mega-lemonade venture, with franchises to be offered, initially in the United States and, within two years, worldwide.

As we were all having milk and cookies to celebrate, who should walk in but the Alfinis, from around the corner. Of course, the Alfinis are both lawyers. We told them about the venture and Mr. Alfini pointed out that the opening of a commercial venture on the sidewalks of residential neighborhoods violates the zoning ordinances.

As the group was falling into deep despair, Mrs. Alfini reminded everyone that she is on the city zoning board and, for a ten percent slice of the lemonade venture, thought she could do a pretty good job of presenting our case for a variance.

This report is getting too long, so I'm going to end it right now.

Think I'll Make Me A Lawyer or Two

DO YOU LIKE RIDDLES? Well, here's one for you.

I manufacture lawyers. I shape their reputations. I arrange and break up marriages. I work on a contingency fee basis. Lawyers pretend that I don't exist. Who am I?

Manufacture lawyers. You're probably thinking law school dean or professor. Wrong. They manufacture law *graduates*, not lawyers.

Shape their reputations. Legal publications? Could be.

Arrange and break up marriages. Now you're thinking matrimonial lawyer, aren't you?

Contingency basis. Must be a personal injury lawyer.

Pretend I don't exist. Secretary? Client?

In any case, it certainly looks like we're talking about at least five different people. But we're not. We're talking about one. Me. Craig Zibrewski, headhunter extraordinaire.

Lawyers are my inventory. Like I said, I manufacture them. I put them on the shelf. I collect them. I sell them. I trade them. Where they don't exist, I create them.

What a business. I love it. Let me tell you how it came about. How it grew. How it changed. How it works.

Unlike most manufacturing businesses, mine is not capital intensive. In fact, you can set up shop with just a telephone and a phone book. Oh sure, a few other things might come in handy, but they're not necessary.

Okay, so let's say you've decided to become a headhunter; you've taken the big plunge, invested in a phone. What's next? Dial an attorney. Who? Doesn't matter; you've got to start somewhere, so just go ahead and dial. Let's play it out, here goes:

"Hello."

"Hello. Mr. Jackson?"

"Yes."

"Mr. Jackson, this is Craig Zibrewski, of ExecuMatch. I'm glad I caught you in. May I call you Jim?"

"You may if you like, but my name's Bill."

"Bill, sorry about that. Look, I need to talk to you on a confidential basis, is that okay?"

"Sure."

"Bill, confidentially, you've got a terrific reputation in your field, and I have several firms who would be very interested in your hooking up with them. Now I know that you're not looking for a new position, but that's just the kind of person my clients are looking for: somebody who is not looking. And the more you are not looking for a position, the better my clients like you. Bit of irony there, I think.

"Anyway, let me ask you this: Can you imagine being more content than you are now, making quite a bit more money, working with people who appreciate your contribution more than your current firm?"

"Yes, I suppose that would be possible."

"I thought so. Well, look then, Bill, you owe it to yourself to explore these opportunities, on a confidential basis, of course. Now here's my address. Just send me twenty or thirty copies of your resume, and be sure to mark the envelope 'confidential.' Now do you have any friends of similar quality who are also definitely not looking, but who might be interested in exploring an unusual opportunity—substantial pay increase, big clients, top lawyers, fast growing firm? . . . Good, now do you happen to have their phone numbers handy?"

That's it. Congratulations, you did it. Simple as that, you're in the legal headhunting business. You've manufactured your first lawyer. Now, of course, once you get Bill's resume, you're going to have to find some firms that may be interested in him and his friends. But that should be a piece of cake.

There have been those who would question the ethics of the business I just described. After all, you have held out some positions that you don't have. But you *will* get them. And if you don't, who's been harmed? All you're doing is creating greater liquidity in the attorney marketplace. What could be more American than that?

You might be surprised that talented attorneys, like Bill, who represent the who's who of corporate America in multi-billion dollar transactions, would be so ready to ship off their resumes to somebody they don't even know. But, hey, who among us thinks he's really valued the way he ought to be in his job? And who isn't looking to better himself, if he can? And doesn't everybody like to be told he's desirable? So why are you surprised?

Now, of course, with the low barriers to entry, the big cash payoff if you make a match and the need of the legal market for bodies, the headhunter industry boomed. Pretty soon me and my cohorts were talking to large numbers of lawyers looking to make lateral moves. And, since we were in the business, they looked to us for information about the law firms they were interviewing with. So we began to manufacture not only lawyers, but the reputations of the law firms at which we were placing those lawyers.

At the same time, partners in the firms we were working with regarded those of us in the headhunting business as, to use a technical term, sleazeballs. As such, despite the fact that they were relying on us to staff their manpower needs, to fuel their growth, the brilliant partners at these prestigious firms refused to return our phone calls and treated us like dirt. Not surprisingly, the firms whose partners did that found that their reputations in the legal marketplace plummeted.

About this time, some of us headhunters looked at the economics of what we were doing and came to a few conclusions that started to change the nature of our business. In the early years we were, for the most part, shuffling relatively young associates. For that, we were paid a percentage of the annual salary of the associate, typically 25% or 30%. Now, if the associate were paid, say, $80,000, that meant that we would pocket $20,000 to $24,000 per placement. What, we asked ourselves, would happen if we placed a partner, whose annual salary might be three or four times that of the associate? Why, we answered, seems like we would make three or four times the money. And what if we placed a group of attorneys whose combined salaries were ten or twelve times the salary of a single associate?

So we began making marriages (or mergers, as they were called). And when those mergers fell apart, we placed people out of the firms we'd put them into in the first place. This was an awful lot of fun. And extremely profitable. But what the heck, law firms were making a lot of money, too, so they didn't seem to mind.

But then the legal market turned south. Economics got bad. Firms weren't hiring many new people. They weren't looking for laterals. In fact, they were looking to get rid of lawyers. They were downsizing, outplacing—er, firing.

Well, naturally, we headhunters were sad to see that happen. But gosh darn if it didn't seem to present a business opportunity for us, again. If firms wanted outplacement, we'd outplace for them. If what goes up must come down, we thought, maybe what comes in must go out.

And, what with law firms hitting on hard times, it occurred to us that those firms might just need some advice. With us being in touch with so many lawyers and law firms, who knows more about them than we do? Since the consulting business has about the same barriers to entry as the headhunting business used to, we got ourselves another telephone—and became consultants. So now those partners who wouldn't return our phone calls a couple years ago are paying us fancy hourly rates for our advice. Or they're asking us to help them move someplace else. It's a wonderful world, isn't it?

So, as you can see, there've been quite a few ups and downs in the economy of the legal profession in the last couple of decades. In fact, you might say that the profession has been something of a bucking bronco. And we headhunters have been holding on for dear life, with both arms wrapped around our lawyers' necks. Yahoo!

'Round the World

HIRAM MAUER, president of Telecom Gigantic, left on a trip around the world with his wife, Loretta, just as negotiations for the purchase of his company by AT&T reached the crucial stages. He left matters in the hands of his executive vice president, Felicia Albion, and his long-time corporate attorney at Fairweather, Winters & Sommers, T. William Williams. The following is taken from the Fairweather correspondence files:

June 28, 1994

Dear Hiram:

Hope you and Loretta crossed the pond safely, and are off to a good start on your trip. I hate to bother you, but an issue has arisen that warrants your immediate attention.

As you know, the purchase price for Gigantic contemplates a base amount, plus a payout tied to Gigantic's income over the next five years. AT&T has taken the position that income is to be reduced by (a) depreciation on capital equipment, (b) a reserve for bad debts, (c) amounts attributable to increased revenue generated from existing AT&T customers who were not customers of Gigantic, and (d) amounts attributable to decreased revenue to AT&T due to the acquisition of Gigantic.

While AT&T insists on all four deductions, we may be able to convince them to back off, if I take a tough negotiating position.

I am of the opinion that a reasonable compromise would be for us to agree to the deduction of (a) and (b) above, but not to the deduction of (c) and (d) above. Felicia thinks that we should agree to (b) and (c), but not (a) and (d). My paralegal thinks that we should agree to (b) and (d), but not (a) and (c). Please advise as to which position you wish us to take. I will not bother you again, unless absolutely necessary.

While you are in London, be sure to see Buckingham Palace (where the queen lives).

Sincerely,

T. William Williams

* * *

July 18, 1994

Dear T-Bills:

Regarding your letter of June 28, don't agree to any deductions from income.

Thanks for the tip on Buckingham Palace.

We're off to Venice.

Loretta sends warm greetings.

Sincerely,

Hiram Mauer

July 29, 1994

Dear Hiram:

Glad you liked the palace.

I've presented your position to AT&T. They argue that deduction of depreciation is warranted to recognize that you are slowly consuming an asset that they will have to replace; that bad debts should be deducted since, historically, you have not collected all of your receivables and that your income would therefore be overstated; that amounts attributable to their customers should not be included since this is revenue that they would have received in any event; and that reductions in their income attributable to you should be deducted since they should be paying you only for the net benefit that you bring to them in the transaction. They asked that I ascertain your reasons for denying these deductions.

I sense that they may be willing to compromise, but feel that this point may be a deal breaker. Sorry to bother you again, but this seems important.

While you are in Venice, be sure to take a gondola ride.

Awaiting your instructions, I remain

Yours sincerely,

T. William Williams

August 23, 1994

Dear T-Bills:

Tell them I don't want those deductions because they're going to reduce the purchase price that I'll be paid, and I'd rather not do that.

The gondola ride was a super idea.

We sail for Greece day after tomorrow.

Loretta sends a hug.

Keep up the good work.

Sincerely,

Hiram Mauer

* * *

August 31, 1994

Dear Hiram:

Thought you and Loretta might like that gondola ride.

I'm afraid we're running into a real problem with the purchase agreement. AT&T seems adamant about deducting at least the depreciation. They say that it would be unheard of to calculate the income without taking depreciation into account, that it would be unfair not to do so, that they have always deducted depreciation in all of their purchase agreements and that their board of directors would never approve an agreement that did not call for depreciation to be deducted.

I must advise you that deduction of depreciation would not be at all unusual in this sort of agreement and that since they have apparently agreed to drop their other demands because of the tough negotiating posture I've taken, it would seem to me to be a reasonable compromise for us to agree to their request. Felicia has authorized me to say that she concurs in my view. In any event, it appears that if we do not agree to this provision, the deal will collapse, so I thought it prudent to trouble you once more.

Please instruct me how you wish to proceed.

Try to pop by the acropolis while you're in Athens.

Yours most sincerely,

T. William Williams

* * *

September 9, 1994

Dear T-Bills:

Marvelous little hill, the Acropolis. How do you uncover all of these out-of-the-way spots?

You're doing just fine with the agreement. Continue to decline to agree to any deductions from income.

We leave for Moscow next Thursday.

Loretta sends love.

Sincerely,

Hiram Mauer

September 18, 1994

Dear Hiram:

Thought you and Loretta might enjoy the acropolis. We came across it in a guidebook (apparently quite a popular book, since the hill was absolutely mobbed the day we were there).

AT&T has made what they say is their last and final offer. They say that although they have never done this before, they will agree to deduct only one-half of the depreciation from income. They say that they are offering this in a spirit of compromise and good will, and hope and trust that this will allow us to finalize the agreement. Both Felicia and I recommend that you accept this offer and authorize us to complete the agreement.

While you are in Moscow, you and Loretta should stop at a Mexican restaurant called El Taco Loco. I think the address is 143 Provisgradsky. The guacamole is out of this world.

Awaiting word, I remain

Most sincerely,

T. William Williams

* * *

October 1, 1994

Dear T-Bills:

The guacamole at the Loco was the culinary highlight of our trip.

Reject AT&T's last and final offer.

We leave for Tokyo on the 10th.

Loretta sends kisses.

If you get back to Russia, try visiting the Kremlin (we heard about it in Fodor's).

Sincerely,

Hiram Mauer

* * *

October 18, 1994

Dear Hiram:

Thought you'd love that guacamole.

I've relayed your position to AT&T and, although they assure me they have never agreed to a formula that does not deduct depreciation, they have decided to accede to what they still believe is your unreasonable position in the interests of resolving this and concluding the agreement. I am now proceeding to finalize the agreement, which should be ready for your signature upon your return.

As long as you're in Tokyo, you and Loretta should try some of that raw fish they make—I think it's called gucci.

Sincerely,

T. William Williams

November 1, 1994
Via FAX

Dear T-Bills:

Your negotiating skills have paid off handsomely. Please discontinue all work on the AT&T purchase agreement. I've run into a Japanese businessman who's offered me $200,000,000 more than AT&T for Gigantic. We have a handshake deal, and that's good enough for me. We can take care of any legal niceties when I get back after the first of the year.

Loretta sends a big smooch.

Sincerely,

Hiram Mauer

P.S. The loafers were delicious.

Conflicting Advice

THE FAIRWEATHER, WINTERS & SOMMERS Clients Association met Thursday last, at the request of the Fairweather Executive Committee, to discuss the sticky issue of conflicts of interest. Jack Rite told those gathered that the Executive Committee had asked the FCA to develop a policy statement on conflicts of interest, and to propose a method for the firm to handle them.

"I don't understand why this is such a sticky issue in the first place," said Ben-Ben. "If there's a conflict, you just avoid it."

"For ethical reasons?" asked Rebecca Fissure.

"No, for financial reasons. If you take a case involving two clients, one of the firm's clients will be bound to lose, and therefore would be unhappy and might take his business elsewhere."

"Maybe," said Jack, "but it's equally true that one of the Fairweather clients would win, and therefore would be happy. This guaranteed 50-50 winning percentage is considerably better than the firm's clients have been faring of late against non-firm clients, at least if my experience is typical."

Rebecca said that both Ben-Ben and Jack had missed the point. The issue was larger than whether permitting conflicts of interest would increase or decrease the firm's success rate; the Code of Professional Responsibility, by which she, as corporate counsel, and all members of the Fairweather firm were bound, prohibited conflicts.

Ben-Ben opined that conflicts of interest had been blown up way out of proportion of late. Anybody who had more than one client had the possibility of a conflict of interest. "For example," he explained, "let us suppose that we have a lawyer, we'll call him X in order to be discreet, although we all know his name is not really that. Anyway, X has two clients; we'll call them F and N. F does not know N, nor does N know F. In fact, F lives in South Dakota (near Woonsocket) and N lives in Alabama (in Slocomb). Is there a conflict of interest?"

Rebecca waved her hand frantically and was recognized by Ben-Ben. "I don't want to appear to jump to conclusions, but I don't see any conflict here," she ventured.

"Aha, you have fallen into a trap that many otherwise scrupulous lawyers have wandered into in the past," said Ben-Ben. "The correct answer to my question is 'potentially, yes.' To see this clearly, let us suppose that F is on his way to visit his failing Aunt Edna in Kenansville, N.C. and, about the same time, N leaves Slocomb for a long weekend in Bailey's Harbor, Wis., where his wife (Mrs. N) attended high school. What happens? Well in Morton's Gap, Ky., in a driving rain storm, BOOM!, F and N collide. Several hundred dollars of damage is done to F's Chevy Nova (blue), and N's jaw is broken when it hits F's fist in the argument that ensues. Can X represent both of his clients, F and N, in the ensuing litigation? I suggest to you that the answer is a resounding, 'NO!' And yet, should X be faulted for getting himself into this conflict of interest? Probably not."

Jack asked Ben-Ben what the point of his story was.

Ben-Ben said the point was that everything in life was not so crystal clear as it sometimes appeared and also that people who live in glass houses should pull the blinds. A distinction should be drawn between actual and potential conflicts of interest. Clearly the FCA should advise the Fairweather Executive Committee to proscribe all actual conflicts, but not all potential conflicts. The question was when does a potential conflict become serious enough to rise (or waft up) to the level of a conflict in the ethical sense.

Leonard Jenkins objected that Ben-Ben's formulation, while neat, was too simple. "Not even all actual conflicts need be avoided," he suggested. A collective gasp escaped the chest cavities of the other FCA members. "Follow along with me," Leonard bade them. "In the same hypothetical, let us suppose that the cars of F and N did not collide. Rather, let us assume that F skidded off the road into a lamp post. F sues General Motors, claiming that a faulty engine in the Nova caused the accident. F comes to X and asks him to file a class action on behalf of himself and all other Chevy Nova owners who have had similar accidents. Is there a conflict of interest?"

Rebecca answered, "That's simple. Since they missed each other, there is no conflict. X does not represent General Motors."

"Aha!" said Leonard. "Again you have jumped too quickly. You forgot to inquire whether X has prepared a will for N."

"What the hell does that have to do with this fact situation?" asked Rebecca.

"Plenty. It turns out that X has, in fact, prepared a will for N and therefore knows that N has 100 shares of General Motors stock. Thus, the lawsuit that X has been asked to file on behalf of F will directly and adversely affect N, if it is successful. Still, although N will be affected directly, his interest is so small that I would say that X could safely take on the case without fear of being criticized."

"True, perhaps," said Rebecca, "but the answer might well be different if N had 100,000 shares of General Motors, or if his General Motors stock constituted a substantial part of his net worth, and the potential outcome of the suit were material to General Motors."

Jenkins said that he thought Rebecca had a point. "The question is not whether the conflict is direct or indirect, but whether it is material or immaterial."

"That's right," said Rebecca. "I knew I had a point. But my point is that what's material for one is not necessarily material for another. Therefore, that distinction doesn't really help."

Jack said it appeared that, thus far, they had determined that not every potential conflict was a conflict and that what's material to one is not necessarily material to another. While all of that certainly was helpful, he said, it did not give the firm the type of litmus test the Executive Committee was fervently hoping for. Perhaps, he suggested, the association should take a different tack altogether.

Ben-Ben thought that the Jack's suggestion was an excellent one. He always had found it useful, he said, when he seemed to be bumping up against a stone wall to start over again, rather than to keep on butting up against it. A fresh look at things could often make all the difference in the world.

Jack thanked Ben-Ben for his support. "I think our trouble is that we've been approaching this like lawyers, which is why the lawyers at the Fairweather firm couldn't resolve the issue in the first place. All of the analyses we have suggested are far too lawyerlike—actual-potential, direct-indirect, material-immaterial. A conflict of interest is a very practical matter. It has to do with how we, the clients, feel, not with nice legalistic distinctions. What lawyers are really saying is that they don't want to do anything that is going to piss us clients off.

"So what the Fairweather firm ought to do when a potential conflict comes along is hire a bunch of us clients and wire us up for EKGs. They would then tell us the fact situation, have us pretend that we are the clients in that situation, and if our hearts go crazy, the firm would know there's a conflict in the ethical sense. Over time, the firm could develop tests as to what degree of fibrillation is required to constitute a prohibited conflict, and what just requires the firm to sit down and talk a bit with the client."

"So what should we tell the Fairweather Executive Committee?" asked Rebecca.

"Well, since it turns out that what they really need is some scientific data, this is clearly beyond the jurisdiction and ken of the Fairweather Executive Committee," said Ben-Ben. "Why don't we recommend that the matter be referred to a newly-created committee to deal with technological methods for resolving legal issues?"

[EDITOR'S NOTE: The conflicts matter is now pending before CHEAT, the new FWS Committee Handling Ethics and Technology.]

In-House or Out-House?

TWO MONTHS AGO, Rebecca Fissure, former Fairweather associate and now general counsel of Cellular Solutions, convened a meeting of her legal department, which had grown to five lawyers. Below is a transcript of a portion of that meeting.

"As you know, the purpose of this meeting is to review the status of our relationships with outside counsel," Rebecca started. "I am continuing to get pressure from the top to control our legal costs."

"I think the problem is we've got too many outside law firms," offered Frank Habler. "We've got one for patent work, one for tax, another one for litigation, one for corporate work, another one for environmental compliance, still another for antitrust. . ."

"Frank's right," chimed Sharyn Tepper. "If we had fewer law firms, we could negotiate better fee deals with them."

"I doubt that," offered Ed Felser. "After all, we run these beauty contests for almost every new matter that comes along, so we know we're getting the best price available."

"I don't think running those contests means we're getting the best price at all. In fact, I think they probably increase the cost we pay," said Frank.

"How do you figure that?" asked Ed. "According to the Constitution, or something equally authoritative, the more competition you get, the lower the price. What are you, some kind of Commie-pinko-Marxist?"

"Heavens, no. But by holding these contests, we've introduced an inefficiency into the marketplace."

"What kind of inefficiency?"

"The contests themselves. To compete, firms have to prepare a presentation, design fancy brochures and proposals, and spend hours of their senior lawyers' time appearing before us."

"Yes, but we don't get charged for that time, do we?"

"If you mean do we see a line on our legal bills that says, 'preparation for beauty contest, attendance at beauty contest, etc.' the answer is 'no'."

"See, so it's free."

"Wait a minute. All lawyers have to sell is their time, right? So if we are making law firms spend their time doing presentations for us, the cost of that time has got to come back to haunt us in some fashion, probably in the form of higher hourly rates."

"So you mean those firms are getting us to pay for the silly hoops we're making them jump through in order to get our legal work?"

"You got it, Ed."

"Why, those sneaky so-and-sos."

"But what about when we get a flat guaranteed fee on a matter, Frank? They don't get to sneak in those costs then, do they?" asked Jon Asquit.

"Sure they do. What do you think those fixed fees are based on—the inflated hourly rates of their lawyers."

"I guess you're right, but with a flat fee at least we know what it's going to cost us."

"Yes, we know what it's going to cost us, we just don't know what the 'it' is."

"What are you talking about?"

"We get a flat fee alright, but let's say it's for a piece of litigation. You were in a large law firm, weren't you, Jon?"

"Sure."

"Well, you remember the way you'd dig into a problem and explore all aspects of it to make certain you were giving the client every advantage."

"Of course."

"When you were doing that, you were being paid by the hour, so you knew you'd be compensated for your time, didn't you?"

"Why, Frank, I'm surprised at you. Surely you're not suggesting that a firm that agrees to a flat fee will not explore all issues thoroughly, are you?"

"Let's just say that there may well be a few more stones left unturned."

"And those are our stones, aren't they?"

"You might say so."

"So the flat fees we're negotiating may wind up being a flat fee for a product that's inferior to the one we'd get on an hourly basis?"

"I'm afraid you're right."

"It's like I said, we should be going back to relying on one firm, the way we used to," said Sharyn.

"We can't do that," argued Ed.

"Why not? It served clients fine for over a hundred years," pointed out Frank.

"But law was so much simpler then," argued Ed.

"What's that supposed to mean?"

"That, back then, there weren't so many specialties. It was possible for one firm to represent a client in all areas."

"The law may have become more complex, but so have law firms. They've gotten so much bigger that they now have people to cover all of the areas. So you can still deal with one firm, if you want to," said Sharyn.

"Yes, and that way you can negotiate a favorable fee arrangement with them, covering all of the work," added Jon.

"I'm afraid we won't save much on legal fees by using one firm," said Frank.

"Why not? If they're getting all of our business, we ought to be able to negotiate a hell of a deal," protested Jon.

"The prices they quote us now are based on the market, so that already has the effect of keeping them down. If we negotiate too good a deal, that's going to cut into their profit significantly."

"So what? That's their problem, isn't it?"

"Ultimately it's ours, too. If their profits drop too significantly, some of their best lawyers are going to go elsewhere. That means that what made the firm attractive to us in the first place, the quality of their lawyers, will be declining."

"So then we just up and take our legal work to the other firm that the partner goes to."

"But they won't all go to one firm, so that means we'll wind up using a whole bunch of law firms again."

"So I guess there's no way for us to save money then, eh, Frank?"

"No, I wouldn't say that at all. I can think of at least two ways."

"Well, c'mon, out with them."

"One way is to concentrate our legal work with one firm."

"Hold it. You just said that we wouldn't save money by using just one law firm."

"No, I said that we wouldn't save legal fees."

"Huh?"

"There are ways of saving us money other than by reducing legal fees."

"For instance?"

"Well, we deal with fifteen or so law firms now, right?"

"Right."

"It takes us a heck of a lot of our time to monitor all of those relationships, doesn't it?"

"Yes, I suppose that's true. If we only had one firm to deal with, that would save us a bunch of time."

"You said you had two ideas, though, what's the other one?" asked the Chair.

"The other one is a little more radical. We have a lot of expertise in dealing with law firms, don't we?"

"I'll say we do."

"And now that we're clients, we know what the consumers of legal services really want, and also what drives them batty."

"That's true."

"And we're all talented lawyers. Most of us worked in large law firms before we came here."

"Will you please get to your point, Frank?"

"I'm getting there. With our knowledge and expertise, we'd be in a perfect position to go out into the market and offer legal services to other corporations. And we could use the money we made from those efforts to reduce the net cost of the legal services we're providing to our own company."

"You mean, just go out and sell our legal services?"

"Exactly."

"We couldn't do that," objected Jon, "it'd be a conflict of interest."

"Oh, we'd figure out some way to get around that. Maybe form a separate subsidiary or something."

"You've got to be kidding," said the Chair.

"Why, it'd work, I tell you," said Frank. "We could compete with any law firm out there."

"I'm not suggesting we couldn't compete," said the Chair. "But if we were successful, we'd find ourselves back in the thick of the hustle and bustle of law firm practice. And that's what we came to this legal department to avoid, remember?"

Oyez, O-No

BEFORE ASCENDING TO THE BENCH . . . That's rather peculiar, isn't it . . . ascending. Why ascending? Well, I suppose that most judicial seats *are* elevated, so that, in a purely physical sense, when you become a judge, you do ascend.

But, of course, ascension is more than just a physical phenomenon. So when I was selected a judge, to be candid, I felt my social position had ascended as well.

I suppose it all goes back to law school, the desire to be a judge, I mean. You are taught that becoming a judge is the pinnacle of the profession. You imagine yourself a Holmes, Brandeis, Frankfurter or Marshall in the way you imagined yourself a DiMaggio, Mays or Duke Snider as a kid. You see yourself assuring equal justice for all, writing opinions with the odd pithy phrase, striding, robed, into your courtroom as all rise to acknowledge your presence. So, when the call came, I didn't hesitate to say I'd take the position.

And, to some extent anyway, my expectations have been fulfilled. I have to admit that I enjoy being called "your honor." Who wouldn't? But now that I've been a judge for a couple years, I also have to admit that I often find myself wishing I were just a plain old lawyer again.

Why? Well for starters, part of me loves the irresponsibility that comes with being a lawyer. As a lawyer, you take sides. You don't have to worry much about who's right. Oh, of course, in some sense you do. You have to evaluate a case or situation, make some judgment about the risks, the likely outcomes. But, ultimately, it's up to somebody else to decide—sometimes the client, sometimes the judge.

Me, I don't have that luxury. I've got to decide. And, of course, if I'm wrong, there's somebody who is happy to tell me so: the appellate court. You don't want to be told you're wrong too often by those folks. And they don't always have the nicest way of pointing out your errors to you. Recently, one of my brethren had an appeals court say, "While ordinarily the trial court is entitled to a large amount of discretion in regard to its assessment of the evidence presented to it, the assessment of the trial court in this case is so far outside of any scope, however large, to which it might be entitled, that we unanimously and emphatically reject each of its findings, and reverse." That smarts a bit.

I guess it's true what they say about the grass always being greener. When I was practicing law, I used to resent it when a judge failed to take into consideration a scheduling conflict I had (typically a long-standing golf date). It always seemed to me that I was at the whims of both my clients and the court. What I didn't realize was that while as a lawyer my work would ebb and flow with the demands of my clients, as a judge there would be a never-ending stream of work. In effect, I had an unlimited number of clients, none of whom could I talk back to, none of whom could pay me directly and none of whom could even take me out for a round of golf. Talk about the worst of all possible worlds.

Now I don't want to be one of those people who slings mud at the profession to which I still belong, but let's just say that my perspective has changed a bit. I used to marvel at the inability of judges to "get it," to understand the nuances of the case in front of them. That no longer seems so strange to me.

After all, what have we got? Two sides represented by the best legal advice money can buy, each trying to convince the poor judge that there's only one way to see the case. If that were really true, it's unlikely that the best legal advice that money could buy would each have advised their clients to proceed with the matter in the first place.

But that's just for starters. In a big case, you may have teams of eight or ten lawyers per side, each focusing their entire attention on the matter, expending whatever resources are necessary. From the judge's side, you've got one judge with an inexperienced law clerk assisting him, for whom the case in front of him is one of several hundred on his docket. That makes it somewhat less shocking that the parties have a richer understanding of the nuances of a case than the judge.

I say we've got to do something to remedy this imbalance, before the courts become just like the post office. What do I mean by that? Well, when was the last time you got anything important through the regular mail? Ten years? Longer? Private delivery services, fax machines, and electronic mail have preempted use of the postal service for everything but junk mail.

Well, the same thing is happening to the courts. Private dispute resolution groups are skimming off the best cases and resolving them more quickly for a lot less money than we can. Why are they able to do that? Simple. They do not have to take the highly unprofitable stuff—small cases, criminal trials. They do not have the huge fixed costs that come with elaborate courtroom buildings and staff. And they have parties who seem more genuinely interested in resolving than in prolonging their disputes. I'm afraid that our court cases have become the junk mail of the legal system.

What can we do about it, you ask? I reckon there are at least two alternatives. First, we could privatize the court system. We could recognize that the federal government just can't compete, government should get out of the justice business. Now, to be sure, there are some small constitutional problems with this approach, what with Article III and all. But we can't just sit there and hide behind the Constitution. The damn thing's over two hundred years old, anyway. No wonder the darn thing doesn't work. Call a constitutional convention. Bring everyone to Philadelphia. If the thing needs changing, I say, let's fix it up.

Now I said that there were two alternatives. The second does not even necessitate amending the Constitution. It would simply involve outlawing all private dispute resolution mechanisms. You might argue that this is protecting an inefficient means of handling a problem by imposing regulation where none is necessary or desirable. Maybe. But isn't that what government is all about?

And, besides, do you know what some of those alternative resolution dudes are making? Big bucks, I'll tell you that, *big* bucks. And those of us on the bench have to beg for the paltry salary increases we manage to get pushed through periodically. Oh, sure it's nice to be called "your honor" and "may it please the court" and all of that stuff. But that doesn't exactly put bread on the table. I didn't think the money would be a big deal to me when I took the bench, but I didn't reckon with sitting up here day after day, looking down at lawyers with one-tenth my ability making six times what I make.

Sure the thirty-year-old kid has to call me "your honor," but I know what that little smart aleck's thinking when he's arguing his motion in front of me: "You may be able to grant or deny this motion, but I'm making twenty grand a year more than you are right now—whichever way you rule—and the salary differential between us is only going to grow each year. So go ahead and rule any way you want, you old geezer; even if you rule against me, I'll appeal."

Now, maybe you think I've become obsessed with money, given up the principles and values that led me to take this position in the first place. Sure, that would be just like you, wouldn't it, just demean me further. Well, it won't work. Because I'm above that. I'm above the pettiness that used to beset me as a lawyer. I've ascended to the bench, don't forget that. No, don't forget that for a second. Because you may have the money, but just remember that I've got some power, and I'm not afraid to use it. I don't want you to think that I would ever do it in an unfair or vindictive manner. No, I'd never do that. But remember that if you high-priced hired guns can't agree on what the law is, a judge can pretty much come down any way he wants to and still be outside the ambit of reversible error, so, if I were you, I'd just watch my step, buster.

Divorce, American Style

PSYCHIATRIST FELIX TAFT dictated the following notes of his most recent session with Amelia Cruthers, a relatively new patient of his who is suffering through protracted divorce proceedings.

Ms. Cruthers arrived at my office last Tuesday, April 24, sobbing and smoking two cigarettes. Her hair was disheveled and she appeared to have been drinking rather heavily. I asked whether she'd been in another argument with her husband, Bobby. She shook her head "no" and began mumbling "book of records, book of records" repeatedly. I asked her where she had been and what she was talking about.

She said, "fair weather, book of records, winter, summer." I asked her to please get hold of herself and tell me what was going on so I could try to help her.

At that point she regained control of herself and became more coherent. "I've been to my lawyer, Penelope Pincher, at Fairweather, Winters & Sommers," she said. "This divorce of mine has been dragging on for almost seven years now. The way it's going, I'll wind up in the Guinness Book of Records. I can just see it:

> Amelia Cruthers — Longest divorce proceeding: 27 years. Largest proportion of attorneys' fees to settlement: 19:1.

"I can't understand what's holding things up," Amelia continued. "It's not the kids, that's for sure. Mandy and Joe were both in high school when this thing started, but now Mandy's married and Joe's engaged—and they both have better jobs than I do.

"And there isn't all that much property involved. We've worked out the stickiest issue: custody of Tater. The dog. Tater's 'bout the only thing that kept Bobby's and my marriage together the final two years."

I asked Amelia how she and Bobby had managed to resolve custody of Tater.

"Joint custody," she said. "He'll be with Bobby Friday through Sunday, and with me Monday through Thursday. Bobby gets him for Thanksgiving and New Year's, and I get him for Armistice Day and the Jewish holidays."

But neither of you is Jewish, I pointed out to Amelia.

"No," she conceded, "but Penny, my lawyer, has an allocation of minors for the Jewish holidays provision in her form custody agreement, so I get Tater for Rosh Hashannah, Yom Kippur, Purim and the first two nights of Pesach.

"We each get Tater for four weeks during the summer, but neither of us can take him out of the country without the consent of the other. Penny insisted on the restriction against taking Tater out of the country because a client of hers once got burned badly."

I asked her what she meant by that.

Amelia explained, "Penny was representing my friend, Judy Elliot, in her divorce from her husband, Vito, and she worked out a joint custody arrangement for Judy and Vito's parrot, Atsanice. But Vito took Atsanice and flew the coop, all the way to Rio. In fact, it was sort of a miracle that Judy ever found him.

"Vito was a diplomat from Italy. After the divorce, he got transferred to the Italian embassy in Brazil and kept Atsanice in his office there. Fortunately, somebody heard Atsanice speaking English at the Italian embassy in Rio and got suspicious.

"Judy tried to have the custody decree enforced in Brazil, but it got pretty expensive. Penny had to hire local counsel in Rio. And Judy also had to pick up half the cost of a court-appointed lawyer for Atsanice, because the Brazilian court determined that that's what the state court in the U.S. would have done in a child custody case. They also ordered Atsanice to undergo a psychiatric evaluation to help the court determine what would be in the parrot's best interest.

[NOTE TO FILE: potential new line of business. Check whether any courts here appoint psychiatrists in pet custody contests. Find out how to get on referral lists.]

I told Amelia that I thought this was a terribly sad story, but I assumed that eventually Judy got Atsanice back.

"Actually, she didn't," Amelia told me. "Atsanice testified at trial that he was much happier in Rio because he had developed a romantic attachment to a cockatoo belonging to the Swedish consul general. Of course that was tragic for Judy. It broke her heart. But Penny took it pretty hard, too, because Judy refused to pay her attorney's fees. But as Penny said, 'once burned, twice something or 'nother,' so she put the restriction against leaving the country into her form pet custody provision."

I asked Amelia whether, since the custody problem with Tater had been worked out, any other sticky issues remained in the divorce.

Amelia said, "Yes, we still have the dining room table problem to deal with. Bobby and I need to divide up our furniture and our other personal property, and we both want the dining room set. It's not really that special. But it's a matter of principle. Or at least that's what Penny says.

"She thinks I've been too soft in caving into Bobby's demands, and feels I need to put my foot down here. I

pointed out to Penny that that meant that I was now holding up the divorce settlement of a case that's been going on for seven years because of a dining room table I don't care about. Penny said that it did seem a bit extreme when I put it that way, but that, as a lawyer, she believed that principle must be upheld, because once you wavered on principle you were sliding down the slippery slope of something or 'nother."

I asked Amelia whether there might not be some way to settle the dining room table issue.

"We've tried to find a way to compromise. His lawyer suggested cutting the table in half and dividing up the chairs, four-four. And Penny suggested we coordinate the scheduling of our dinner parties and move the set back and forth between us. Sort of the Tater approach to the dining room set, I guess. She'll probably insist on a provision that prevents either of us from taking the dining room set abroad."

At this point Ms. Cruthers began sobbing again and, though I do not normally do this, I began to talk about my own divorce experience. I told her that though Suzy and I have only been separated a few months, I think we've about resolved things. Naturally Amelia asked how we'd managed to do that and so I continued with my story.

"Well, we started out with lists of property, financial records, affidavits, appraisals . . . you know the routine. After a couple months, I got my first bill for legal fees, and I called Suzy up and suggested we have a drink. Turned out, she'd just gotten her first bill, too. Quite a shock the first one, isn't it? I thought my bill had been mixed up with a bill for a merger between IBM and General Electric. And Suzy felt the same way I did about her bill.

"So Suzy and I started talking about our lawyers. Hers told her how I was going to hide some of my assets from her. And mine told me how Suzy was going to try to milk every penny she could out of me. And neither of us believed that, so the more we talked about them, the angrier we got. And the angrier we got about our lawyers, the less angry we seemed to be at each other."

"You don't mean. . ." Amelia interrupted.

"Yup, me and Suzy are back together again," I told her. "And I don't think it ever would of happened if it weren't for our lawyers. We both decided that we'd be damned if we were going to make them wealthy just because of our little spat."

"Atsa nice!" Amelia said with a smile.

Philosophically Speaking

As PART OF ITS FAMOUS luncheon speakers series, the Fairweather Clients Association invited world-renowned philosopher Professor Bertland Fussle to address its members. Below is a transcript of the professor's remarks:

Ladies and gentlemen, boys and girls:
How do you do?
It is a distinct pleasure and an honor for me to be here this afternoon to discuss my important topic with you. Before I begin, though, I would like to thank Sheldon Horvitz of the Fairweather firm for picking me up at the airport and driving me down to the office. It is always a treat for me to reestablish contact with one of my former students. I must admit that I had not recalled that Sheldon was one of my Philosophy 101 students at Princeton University seventeen years ago, though Sheldon seems to have remembered that experience remarkably well. In gratitude for his driving me here (and, frankly, to shut him up), I have agreed to reread his paper entitled *The Ethical Relativity of Kant: Can Right Be Wrong?* though I have told him there is little-to-no hope, at this late date, that I will raise the C-plus grade that I awarded to him in Philosophy 101 to a B-minus.

You have asked me to address you today on the topic "The Lawyer-Client Relationship: A Philosophical View." Before doing that, of course, we must first ask ourselves whether the lawyer-client relationship exists. For if it were to prove to be the case that that relationship did not exist, for me to expound at length on a philosophical view of that relationship would amount to very little more than idle chatter. And we philosophers are nuts-and-bolts-type guys to whom engaging in idle chatter would be quasi-repugnant.

What is a lawyer? What is a client? What is a relationship? Until we have tackled these questions, we cannot, of course, answer the question of whether the lawyer-client relationship exists.

Now I need hardly tell you (but I will) that a lawyer is a person trained in the law who dispenses advice or otherwise provides legal services for a hefty fee. Technically, the fee need not be hefty for the person to be a lawyer, but it nearly always is, so we might just as well recognize that fact, or, as my daughter would say, "get real." (Of course, a certain amount of work is done pro bono—for the good of the bono—but that's not very important, so we can afford to ignore it.) The person rendering the legal services may be a partner, an associate, a member of a corporate law department, a legal aid lawyer, a government lawyer or some other variation of lawyer. Lawyers are classified into phila and species according to their areas of practice and plumage, but we need not delve into that level of detail here.

The client is the poor schmuck who pays the lawyer's hefty fee. Clients come in two types—important clients and regular clients (the nomenclature is borrowed from fast food restaurants, where there are large and regular drinks, but never small ones). We can be pretty darn sure that clients exist because, if they did not, there would not be so damn many lawyers. In other words—we pay fees, therefore they are.

Relationships fall into at least six categories: cozy, strained, respectful, distant, Platonic and inverse. We philosophers generally favor the Platonic, since that was named after one of our own boys. Most lawyer-client relationships, however, tend to be either inverse or strained.

Speaking of Plato, let's pause to contemplate him a bit, if you don't mind. Plato spoke of the man in the cave, and a candle and reflections. "What is the ideal?" Plato would ask all the time. His answer: ask the philosopher-king. Plato was not what we today would call particularly well grounded in reality. In fact, it's because of Plato that when we speak of something incomprehensible we often say, "It's all Greek to me." (In Greece, where Greek seems to come easily, even for very young children, the phrase is "It's all Nova Scotian to me.")

Now, getting back to the question of whether the lawyer-client relationship exists, I'd say, "yes." So assuming, arguendo, that I am correct, how would a philosopher look at the lawyer-client relationship today? Well, there are three ways of looking at that relationship, and I'd like to take them all at once, since to take them one at a time would merely prolong the analysis, and the agony. There is the ideal lawyer-client relationship, the good-enough lawyer-client relationship and the I'm-not-sure-what-the-heck-is-going-on-here lawyer-client relationship. If you look at these three as a totality, what do you get? A microcosm of the macrocosm that we find cross-culturally in virtually all professions today.

Let me illustrate. I went to the dentist yesterday. First thing they did was usher me into the dental hygienist, Rosie (named for the thorn, not the blossom). Rosie announced that it was time to take some x-rays, since it had been several weeks since they had last taken photos of my teeth. After covering my body and neck with protective devices to stop the x-rays from doing me mortal harm—which did not give me much comfort, since they had been taking those photos without that protection for twenty years—she snapped four candid shots of my mouth.

Rosie then proceeded to berate me for the build-up of plaque, accusing me of not brushing and flossing properly. To incent me to do better in the next six months, she commenced to poke sharp instruments into my gums, inviting me to rinse and spit out about a gallon of blood at approximately 30-second intervals. Rosie then spent another half an hour polishing and flossing my teeth, before summoning Dr. Green into the office. Of the minute Dr. Green spent with me, thirty seconds were consumed in washing his hands, twenty seconds in glancing at the x-rays and asking me if I'd like to order a package of four 8x10 color glossies and a dozen wallet-sized, since they'd turned out so well, and the remainder of the time in looking into my mouth and pronouncing me fit.

What has all of this talk about my visit to the dentist got to do with the topic of this speech? you ask. Good question. Probably not much, but it's on my mind, since I just went yesterday and my gums are still killing me. At least we can see that, unlike dentist-patient relationships, lawyers do not poke their heads into their clients' mouths. This may well be for fear that their clients would bite them off, but, whatever the reason, I applaud the difference. On the other hand, lawyers do not give their clients free toothbrushes and dental floss. Though this may be entirely appropriate, I feel that lawyers should at least consider handing out small legal pads and pens with the firm's name on them.

You know, I once considered going to law school myself. I even went so far as to take the law boards and apply. And I think I would have made quite a fine lawyer, if I do say so myself. Because the law is not entirely devoid of philosophical content, as you well know. To pick just one example, take the famous case of *Environmental Protection Agency* v. *Ferris*. In that case, the EPA sued Ferris, who owned a vast plot of land on which a forest was located. Ferris had been cutting the trees for timber at night, when nobody was around, and the EPA sought an injunction prohibiting the cutting. Ferris defended, claiming that if a tree fell in the forest and nobody was there, it did not make a noise. The court not only held for the EPA, but had Ferris committed to the local Home for the Philosophically Deranged.

I could cite many other examples in which law and philosophy meld, of course, but what would be the point? And the same might be said of further discussion of the philosophical view of the lawyer-client relationship—what would be the point? So I think I will take this opportunity to stop talking, and invite any questions you may have.

[EDITOR'S NOTE: the audience burst into spontaneous applause, relieved that the professor had spared them a fuller exposition of his topic. And, except for Sheldon Horvitz's question as to when the professor thought he might complete rereading Sheldon's paper on Kant, the group declined to query Fussle further.]

Ferreting Out What's Fair

MANY CLIENTS have turned to the firm of Ketchem Cheeten Associates, specialists in auditing legal bills, to review the statements for legal fees submitted by Fairweather lawyers. Through careful sleuthing, KCA has saved clients tens, even hundreds, of dollars. Set forth below are portions of the KCA Auditors Guide, used by KCA to train its new auditors, obtained by a Fairweather undercover agent.

INTRODUCTION

Your job is to identify where the law firms you are auditing have overstated their bills. Notice that we don't say *whether* the bills are overstated. That is a given. On average, we find that legal bills are reduced over 31% after our audit. If you are running below that average, chances are that you either are missing some serious padding, or you have become a double agent, working on behalf of the law firm. If you become tempted to succumb to the entreaties of a law firm to work on their behalf, however, you should be aware of the grizzly ends met by some prior defectors.

Double-agent Hector Velture's body was recovered in 2,743 strips when he was accidentally fed through the paper shredder shortly after he was discovered to have disclosed confidential KCA information to a law firm client. Sally Priston met an untimely end when her stomach exploded. An autopsy revealed that she had been force fed all 62 cheese-and-peanut-butter crackers contained in a law firm candy machine. In short, this is not a job for the faint of heart.

While this guide contains many of the techniques used by law firms to inflate their bills, it makes no pretense to having uncovered all of them. Firms are constantly inventing new ways to augment their coffers, so the effective KCA agent must remain ever vigilant, prepared to chase down fraud like a cheetah (pun intended), wherever and whenever it may appear.

Since this book contains the tricks of our trade, you should guard it as if your life depended upon it. It does. Remember Hector and Sally? You will find taped to the back cover of this book a tiny capsule. Should you discover that your copy of the guide has fallen into the hands of the enemy, you may want to swallow this pill. Though it will not prevent the information from being lost, it will provide a quick and relatively painless solution for your predicament. Come to think of it, though, if the guide is stolen, so will the capsule, so you may want to remove the capsule now and insert it in the tape compartment of your pocket dictating machine. No, come to think of it, that's not such a good idea, since you won't be able to dictate. How about behind the sun visor in your car, on the passenger's side?

SCOURING TIME SHEETS

Most of the overbilling you find will come straight from the time sheets you examine. That's where lawyers leave their fingerprints. Here are some situations you are likely to encounter:

1. Lawyer bills more than twenty-four hours in a day. To discover this, normally you will have to obtain copies of the lawyer's time on all matters for the day, since even the

most brazen lawyer will rarely bill more than twenty-four hours to a single matter on a single day. If the lawyer objects to showing you time sheets for the entire day because it might disclose work done for other clients, you may either have the lawyer obliterate the client name on the other matters or simply ask the lawyer whether he wants to be paid for the work he's done.

2. Two lawyers working on a matter attend a meeting; one bills three hours, the other bills four-and-a-quarter hours. Your first tack should be to eliminate the four-and-a-quarter hours altogether, since almost certainly two lawyers should not have attended the meeting in the first place. Assuming that two lawyers were necessary, reduce the four-and-a-quarter hours to three. No lawyer ever understated the amount of time he spent in a meeting. NOTE: advise your client to keep track of the length of meetings they attend with their lawyers so that you can compare those figures with the hours billed on time sheets.

3. Your client is billed for time spent by librarians or other support staff at the firm. Tell the firm that your client hired a *law firm* and it expects to be billed only for time of lawyers. If your client had been interested in engaging the services of a librarian, it would have contacted the American Library Association.

4. Your client is billed for travel time. Tell the firm that you expect that either its lawyers will work for your client while traveling, in which case you will be happy to approve time for the work done, or that its lawyers will work for other clients while traveling, in which case those other clients should have the privilege of paying for the time.

5. Be alert for certain work descriptions, including the following:

>   a. organize file—this is secretarial work; your client should not pay for it

b. review file—this suggests that the lawyer can't remember the matter he's working on; get a new lawyer, or at least don't pay for the time
c. dictate memo to the file—this is a device to protect the lawyer's rear end, and your client should not pay
d. memo to another lawyer in the firm—this probably means too many lawyers are working on the matter, or that one of them is seeking to protect his rear end
e. review and revise bill—not only is your client being billed for the legal work, he's being billed for billing for the legal work and for revising that bill
f. lunch with client—it's bad enough that your client just got socked for the lunch bill, he shouldn't have to pay $250 an hour to listen to his attorney's opinion about the prospects of the Cubs' new third baseman.
g. proofread draft of interrogatories—your client needs to pay a lawyer to proofread? The firm should hire some unemployed college graduate from a prestigious university to do that. The interrogatories are a form document that's been on the firm's word processing system for twenty-three years, anyway. So what does it need proofing for?
h. cite-checked brief—this should be done by the firm's librarian, and not billed to your client.
i. review and redraft letter, memo or document—this often means two attorneys are engaged in revising and re-revising one another's work. The resultant ping pong match becomes a clash of competing literary styles that adds no value to your client.

EXAMINING WORK PRODUCT

Looking over the time sheets may not always reveal the billing problem. For example, you may encounter a time sheet that says, "drafted and revised letter to client—three hours." On the face of it, this may not seem like an inappropriate charge. However, if the letter says, "Dear Joe: Here's a copy of the contract the other side just sent. Regards to Betty," you may want to question why that consumed three hours of lawyer time.

Another example might be charges totaling forty-eight hours for drafting a 100-page real estate sale-leaseback transaction. About two hours a page; sounds like a real steal. Ask to review the firm's form sale-leaseback agreement. You may well find that the forty-eight hours were apparently consumed inserting the names of the parties, their states of incorporation and the date, and deleting the provisions of the agreement that pertain to livery of seisin.

One final example might be a charge of two hours for a memo from one attorney to another. Again, this may appear to be a legitimate charge, until you ask to see the memo, which may read something like the following:

To: Nails Nuttree
From: Helen Laser
Re: *Right* v. *Wrong*

Spoke to our client this afternoon regarding the status of the litigation in *Right* v. *Wrong*. I advised Jim that we had received an offer to settle the litigation for $124,000.

He asked me whether I thought we should accept the offer. I advised him that that was basically a business decision, and that I, as only a lawyer, would not presume to make that business decision for him.

He asked what I thought our prospects were for prevailing on the merits of the case. I told him that while I thought we had a good case, litigation always involved risk, and the other side had its good points, too. I told him that you can never tell what a jury will do with a case like this one, that sometimes you win 'em and sometimes you lose 'em. While $124,000 was not peanuts, neither was it escargot.

Jim thanked me for my input and said he'd get back to me with his business decision in the next couple of days. Please let me know what you think about this.

Note that this memo covers the writer's rear end from attacks both by her client and by her senior partner. You should challenge not only the time recorded for the memo, but also the telephone time spent in giving the client the useless advice. Also, watch for Nails' time in reading and responding to the memo.

EXPENSES

One of the most fertile territories for reducing our clients' legal costs is to examine closely the expenses charged by their attorneys. Many law firm lawyers have the notion that they are royalty, and spend accordingly (except when it's for their own account). Here are a few areas you should be on the lookout for:

1. excessive air travel costs—first-class air travel is for those who can afford it. Your clients cannot. Less visible than first-class fares are coach fares booked on airlines that award attorneys with frequent-flier benefits, but whose fares are higher than those of other airlines. We can discourage that practice in two ways. First, our airline software program automatically calculates the difference between the fare charged to our client and the lowest fare available on other airlines. Second, we advise our clients to require their attorneys to utilize frequent flier miles accumulated on trips for which they pay towards tickets for other flights made on their behalf.

2. charges for photocopying, faxing and the like—while it seems fair for law firms to recoup their costs in expenses, many law firms have established their photocopy, fax and other operations as their principal profit centers. A good rule of thumb is to object to the level of any of these costs, and settle for one-half to two-thirds of the original charge.

3. hotel and meal costs—attorneys view client travel and entertainment as an opportunity to sample the finest hotels and restaurants in the world. Your job is to disabuse them of that notion. Our software program can generate room rates for the nearest Comfort Inn to the hotel the client chose, as well as the median cost of a meal at a local dive. Disallow any lodging or food costs in excess of those generated by our computer.

4. miscellaneous charges—often listed at the end of the bill, miscellaneous expenses generally range from $5 to $20. Because the amounts are so small, clients typically do not contest them. We calculated the total cost of these expenses to our clients last year was $824,585. Disallow all miscellaneous expenses.

[EDITOR'S NOTE: the Fairweather undercover agent who pilfered this guide was found, and is being held captive by KCA agents. He intended to take the poison capsule, but couldn't remember where he'd put it.]

Just a Formality

A CHARMED LIFE I led, until recently that is. My friends, most of them, they're loaded down with lawyers. Divorce, wills, business, houses—you name it. But me, no lawyers in my life. Not a one. None to deal with, none to live next door to; I'm not even related to any. A blessing. Then, all of a sudden, BAM!, and I've got two of them in my life.

Here's how it happened. I'm driving along, must be a year and a half ago now, minding my own business, and BAM!, from behind I'm hit by a guy, Vance L. Winkle III. Honest to God, that's his name. Could I make that up?

Mr. Winkle does not get out of his car immediately. That's because he's on the car phone and has to finish up his call. I wait in my car. I'm hit pretty hard, but I don't think I'm hurt, not badly anyway.

Finally, Mr. Winkle gets out of his car and comes up to me. He apologizes for taking so long, but he's working on this absolutely fascinating legal issue, he explains. It seems his client has been sued for copyright infringement based on selections the client had taken from letters that had been published in the Congressional Record. The letters had been published in his client's book, *Not so Fast, Young Tadpole*, which Rip (by now, Mr. Winkle had told me his nickname) recommended quite highly to me. According to Rip, the letters were clearly in the public domain and therefore not subject to copyright protection. The opposing attorney, on the other hand, was arguing that. . .

At this point I interrupted Rip to remind him that we'd just had an automobile accident. Rip apologized for getting a bit carried away and excused himself to return to his car to phone the police. Not long after that, I heard the sound of a siren and saw the swirling blue light in my rearview mirror.

As Rip and I were providing the police with the details of our accident, a red Cadillac convertible pulled off the road and stopped immediately in front of my car. The occupant of that car, Luigi Petrocellos, was a man I had never met before and have often since wished I had not met then. Luigi, wearing a shiny green suit, sprang out of his Caddy, greeted the police officer by name and introduced himself to me with a flourish, pulling a business card ceremoniously out of the brim of his black fedora and announcing, "Your troubles are over: Luigi Petrocellos is here." I had a sick premonition that my troubles were just about to begin.

Luigi explained that he was an expert in the personal injury field, having once recovered $1.1 million for a client. When I asked the extent of that client's injuries, Luigi pulled from his wallet a string of the most gruesome color photographs it has ever been my displeasure to view. Perhaps sensing my discomfort from the way I bent over, grabbed my knees and uttered retching sounds, Luigi snatched the wallet out of my hands and produced a sheet of paper. "Sign here," he instructed me.

I asked Luigi what it was he was wanting me to sign. "Just a formality," he told me, "so I can represent you."

I read the sheet:

CONTINGENT FEE AGREEMENT

_____ (hereinafter referred to as "The Injured") hereby irrevocably appoints Luigi Petrocellos (hereinafter referred to as "Luigi Petrocellos") as his attorney to act on

The Injured's behalf in connection with any claim arising directly or directly out of _____ (hereinafter referred to as "The Most Unfortunate Calamity").

Luigi Petrocellos shall do Luigi Petrocellos' best to settle any claim arising out of The Most Unfortunate Calamity as quickly as possible, since that's how Luigi Petrocellos makes his dough.

The Injured agrees that Luigi Petrocellos may settle for whatever Luigi Petrocellos thinks is the best deal Luigi Petrocellos can get, even if that isn't all that much.

The Injured shall pay Luigi Petrocellos the full amount of all of Luigi Petrocellos' expenses in connection with attempting to settle The Most Unfortunate Calamity. In addition, The Injured shall pay Luigi Petrocellos one-third of any amount recovered by Luigi Petrocellos on account of The Most Unfortunate Calamity, which amount shall be paid directly out of the settlement, so that Luigi Petrocellos doesn't have to worry about collecting Luigi Petrocellos' fees from The Injured.

If this seems like a sensible way of proceeding, The Injured should put his John Hancock below and Luigi Petrocellos will get on with this.

_____

The Injured

As I looked over the document, I noticed Rip walking towards me again. "What's going on here?" he asked.

I introduced Rip to Luigi Petrocellos and explained that Luigi was proposing to represent me in connection with the accident we'd had. I passed Rip the Contingent Fee Agreement I'd been reading and he perused it quickly. Rip said that he thought legal action would be unnecessary. He was prepared to admit liability and have his insurance company take care of the damage to my car.

That, he thought, should take care of it, since I appeared to be fine.

Luigi took umbrage at this. The damage to my car, he was sure, was far more extensive than Rip's insurance company would recognize. Luigi thought that he had begun to notice a slight limp developing in my walk, and that I was starting to hold my head at an odd angle, signaling to him that I was likely a whiplash victim. Chances were, he thought, I would miss months of work during my painful rehabilitation period, which would entail heavy doses of physical therapy and, most likely, require that I have a whirlpool and exercise equipment installed in my home. Since I looked to Luigi like the type who owned a modest home, all of this would almost certainly mean a two-story addition would need to be built to accommodate all of the new equipment.

Rip thought that Luigi was being ridiculous. I was unlikely to collect on anything other than the damage to my car. And further, Rip pointed out, under the agreement that Luigi had requested I sign, I would relinquish complete control over the settlement of the matter to Luigi. Not only that, Luigi would collect one-third of everything. That meant that if, as Rip suspected, the only damages were the repair of my car and, assuming the repair cost $2,400, Luigi would collect $800, and I would be left to come up with that amount out of my own pocket. So Luigi would add nothing to the settlement, and walk away with one-third of whatever I collected.

As the three of us were speaking, I noticed that other cars had begun to pull off of the road in front of us. Luigi said that it was nonsense to suggest that he would add nothing to the settlement. In fact, Luigi told me, in anticipation of my signing the Contingent Fee Agreement, he had made a few phone calls on his way over to the accident. He grabbed my elbow and walked me up to the

vehicle that had pulled in front of Luigi's Cadillac: a tow truck emblazed with the legend, "Al's Tow and Repair—You Collide, We Fix with Pride."

"This is Al," Luigi told me, pointing to the cigar-puffing lout who extended his grease-filled paw out of the tow truck window towards me. "Al here has the best prices in the area. Nobody charges more than Al. And since your recovery likely will be a multiple of what your out-of-pocket damages are, Al is a good man to have in your corner."

Rip, who had followed us, opined that what Luigi was suggesting was perilously close to fraud. Luigi sneered at Rip and walked me up to the next vehicle in line, an ambulance with the lettering "Safety First Transportation." "After we finish up here at the scene," Luigi explained, "I'm going to have you whisked over to Our Lady of the Whiplashed Hospital—actually it's Saint Mary's Hospital, but we personal injury lawyers made up a little nickname—to have you examined by my friend Dr. Marvin Transplant. Marv is the most conservative doc in the country. He feels that any treatment that's available is a treatment his patient should have, as long as the treatment is painless to the patient, and very expensive. Rip and Luigi exchanged sneers again, as we proceeded up the line.

The next car we came to contained my prospective physical therapist, a pert little redhead named Roxy, the next a dealer in physical therapy equipment by the name of Charlie Brawn, and the last an architect named Eddie Fiss, who specialized in constructing physical therapy additions that could later be converted easily to home entertainment centers.

Rip trailed behind me, listening as we walked up the line of cars Luigi had assembled. With each introduction Luigi made, Rip's eyes seemed to widen. As we left Roxy, the physical therapist, I noticed that Rip appeared to be developing something of a limp; after we left Charlie, the equipment dealer, Rip emitted occasional involuntary "oohs" of pain. And when we'd finished talking to Eddie the architect, Rip asked whether he might have a word with Luigi, in private.

The two of them walked ahead of me and off to the side of the road. I watched in amazement as Rip took out a pen and signed the Contingent Fee Agreement Luigi had been pushing on me. Luigi helped Rip slip into the rear of the ambulance and blew a kiss to Rip as it pulled off. Al hooked Rip's car up to his truck and towed it away. And Luigi laid a strip of rubber as he screeched away after Al in his red Caddy convertible.

I figured that would be the last I'd see of Luigi. But I was wrong. The next day, Luigi popped by my home with another copy of the Contingent Fee Agreement. I questioned how Luigi could represent me against Rip, when he was already representing Rip. Luigi said I had it all wrong. There was no dispute between me and Rip. It was just a couple of insurance companies squabbling. Luigi assured me that he could work everything out just fine for both me and Rip. It was just a formality.

Out on the Beat

BETWEEN ME AND MY next door neighbor, Sheldon Horvitz, we're about a wash; as far as the criminal justice system goes, I mean. Me, I'm a cop. Sheldon, he's a lawyer with Fairweather, Winters & Sommers. I catch criminals; Sheldon gets 'em out. I call Sheldon the pro bono king.

Me and Sheldon get along okay, personally. I lend Sheldon our snow blower, and he'll walk our dog, Rubovits, when we're away for a weekend. Our kids, Stacy and Brian, are best friends; they play together all the time. But when it comes to criminals, me and Sheldon don't exactly see eye to eye.

When I see my daughter, Stacy, and Sheldon's kid, Brian, playing, I think back to how it was for me, when I was growing up. We used to play cops and robbers. We didn't have computer games, or space invaders or nothing, back then. I was poor, and you didn't need a lot of fancy equipment to play cops and robbers. Here was the game: your friends put handkerchiefs over their face, you chased after 'em, caught 'em, cuffed 'em and walked 'em back to the jail, which was under somebody's front porch. Then you switched sides and started all over again.

Seems like things were different when I was a kid. Thieves stole because they wanted money. Maybe they needed to feed their family, maybe they wanted to buy some jewelry or a car or something. Today, they steal for drugs. Oh, sure, there are other reasons, too, but drugs is it, mainly. Seems like bad guys were bad back then because they *wanted* to be. Today it seems like it's out of their control, almost.

Things were simpler, too. There were two sides—cops and robbers. And you knew which were the good guys and which were the bad guys. If you were a kid, playing, you wanted to be the cop, just like if you were playing cowboys and indians, you wanted to be the cowboy.

Today, though, I don't know. I guess kids play cow-persons and native Americans; officers of the law and societally-disadvantaged persons. And you turn on the television and you don't know who the good guy is and who's the bad guy. If the criminal is cool and clever and real bad, then likely as not he's the hero. Or maybe he's grown up unfortunate, had a busted home, a tough life, and that's led him to crime, so the audience winds up rooting for him to get away, or even to kill the cop. Seems all screwed up to me, but what do I know? I'm just a cop.

Actually, just the other day I came home, and Stacy and Brian were really into a new video game. They were each operating a lever that moved a little guy around, and pressing buttons that fired off guns and caused bomb explosions. I hate all that violence in video games. Then, suddenly, after one little video guy captures the other, a bunch of questions and answers pop up on the screen.

After I watched for a while, I asked what they were playing, and Stacy told me, "Cops and Lawyers." It's a game in which the cop goes after a criminal and tries to catch him, then the lawyer tries to get him out. Just like me and Sheldon do, in real life.

In this video game, when the criminal is captured the cop picks a number between one and thirty, and enters it, secretly, into the computer. The lawyer gets three chances to guess what the cop's number is during the rest of the game and, if he guesses it, the computer plays the theme from the movie *Born Free* and the criminal flies away. My daughter explained to me that what was going on was that the lawyer had three continuance shots and, if he hits the cop's unavailability date, the criminal gets out.

After that, both players have to read a story that comes up on the screen about what happened in catching the criminal. The player who plays the lawyer then gets to ask the one who plays the cop a series of twenty-five detailed questions about the story—exact times of events, whether a car had scratches on the passenger-side door, what color shirt somebody wore—and if the cop fails to answer two of the twenty-five questions correctly, the *Born Free* theme plays again and the criminal goes free. If the cop gets all of the answers right, the lawyer gets three appeals and, if he wins any of them, the criminal gets out. Sounds pretty realistic—and scary—to me.

But forget about computer games. From time to time I talk with my neighbor Sheldon about some of the things that bother me in real life. Here's one of them. Guy robs a bank, steals a hundred grand or so. Later the cops get a tip who done it. They go and break into his apartment. Sure enough, stashed away in some drawers is a hundred grand in cash, with the wrappers still around the bills. Looks like we got ourselves a criminal who's going to be spending a bunch of time up the river, right?

Wrong. Some lawyer for the thief figures out that the cops didn't go get a piece of paper saying it was okay to look in the thief's apartment, so they can't use the money they found in the trial and that means they don't have the evidence to convict the thief.

Now there's no question this guy took the dough. It was sitting in his bedroom, for chrisakes. But because somebody didn't get a piece of paper, the thief goes free. Why don't they have some kind of rule that the thief's got to get a piece of paper before he robs the bank and if he don't, then the cops don't have to get no piece of paper, either? I mean, c'mon, what kind of a game are we playing here?

Now when I talk to Sheldon, I ask him does he think this makes sense. He tells me the courts want to make sure the criminal has all of his rights. And so, if they didn't make sure that evidence that was taken illegally couldn't get into court, the cops would not stick to the rules.

Now that don't exactly make sense to me. If the cops don't follow the rules they're supposed to follow, why not lay the punishment on the cops? Isn't it going to make the cops a lot more likely to follow the rules if they suffer some consequences than if the result is that some criminal goes free? After all, who are you punishing? The public, that's who, because they're going to have to deal with this criminal who's on the loose and who sure as hell is going to commit some other crime.

Here's another one I don't understand. You get this guy who shoots his wife, kills her. No question about it. You found the gun, it has his prints on it, you found the body, her blood was on his clothes and you have a motive, they've been fighting over his seeing another woman. And this time the cops have played by all of the rules, so there's no question about the evidence coming in at trial. Looks like an open-and-shut case for murder, right?

Sorry, you're wrong. What happens? Well, the state's attorney decides he's going to plea bargain, so instead of this guy getting a minimum of twenty and a max of the chair, he gets five to ten for manslaughter.

Now, naturally I'm a little curious as to why the prosecutor is going to let this murderer out on the streets again in five years, maybe less with good behavior. The answer is that the defendant has gotten himself a real good lawyer, an experienced trial lawyer from a large law firm who is taking the case on a pro bono basis, and this lawyer's going to try the case to the hilt. He's going to claim insanity and that it was done in the passion of the moment, not planned ahead of time. It's going to take the state's attorney a lot of time to prepare the case and to try it, and the office doesn't have the resources. Besides, there's a chance the state's attorney would lose the case, and that would look very bad in the press. So that led to the plea bargaining, which led to the five-to-ten deal.

So, as I see it, what we got here is the following: We've got a state's attorneys office that isn't set up to try cases. We've got a state's attorney who is afraid to take on a case because he may lose. And we've got a defendant who is able to get top representation for nothing from a big law firm, pro bono publico.

Now, am I nuts or is there something screwy about this? Why is it pro bono publico—for the public good—for a large firm to make sure that a murderer is out on the street in five to ten years? Why wouldn't it be pro bono publico for the firm to supply assistance for the understaffed prosecutor's office so that dangerous criminals would be put away for the full terms they deserve? No wonder I thought I heard the defendant chuckling when he heard his sentence. Maybe that's why they call it "manslaughter," because with a space and an apostrophe you can make it "man's laughter."

So, I guess I get a bit frustrated about the way lawyers mess around in my business. It all seems to be one big game. And the rules don't make no sense to me. I always thought the object of cops and robbers was to catch the robbers, and lock them up. That don't seem to be the object anymore, though. Well, cops and robbers used to be a game for me, too, when I was ten. But it's not a game anymore; it's my life and the lives of a lot of other folks, too. Maybe all this wouldn't bother me quite so much if when I came in the other day Stacy hadn't been fighting with Brian, because she wanted to play the lawyer.

Of Sound Mind and Body

AFTER HER MEETING with Fairweather, Winters & Sommers estate planning ace, Donald Spindle, Shirley Plunkett met her best friend, Rose Goodman, for coffee. The following is a transcription of their conversation.

"Why so glum, Shirley?" asked Rose.

"Harry and I just went to see a lawyer about how to divide up our property."

"You mean you and Harry are getting divorced?"

"Oh, heavens no. We went in to our lawyer, Don Spindle, to redo our wills."

"Oh, that *is* depressing. What made you decide to do that?"

"It had been twenty-six years and six months since we'd signed them, so we thought it was about time.

"How did you know it had been that long?"

"Don sends us a postcard every six months. Here, I have my latest one right here:

Dear Potential Future Decedent:

Did you know that it's now been twenty-six years and six months since your last will or codicil? The American College of Probate Attorneys advises that frequent, periodic revisions to your estate plan is the best way of fighting unnecessary estate and inheritance taxes.

Please call my secretary, Wanda, to arrange for a check-up soon, because we never know what tomorrow may bring.

      Very truly yours,

      Donald M. Spindle

"How did your meeting with Spindle go? What was so depressing about it, anyway?"

"Well, for starters, Don's got this dark, wood-paneled office and he's got all of these framed certificates up on the wall."

"Well, that's fairly standard for lawyers, isn't it: college degree, law degree and the like?"

"Yes, but Don's got a certificate of appreciation from the AMA."

"The American Medical Association?"

"No, the American Mortuary Association. Do you know what their motto is?"

"No, what?"

"We're ready when you are."

"No."

"Yes. The certificate was in appreciation for Don sending his thousandth client their way. And he also had a plaque for being selected the American College of Probate Attorneys' man of the year three years ago."

"That's very impressive. How did he get selected for that?"

"For probating estates that totaled more than $1 billion in that year."

"Well, I can see how he would be very proud of that."

"Yes, I suppose. And then he had all of those plants around the office."

"Well, what's so depressing about plants?"

"They were all dead, except two. And when I asked him why those two looked so good, he told me they were artificial."

"Sounds like the setting left a little something to be desired. How did the meeting go, though?"

"All right, I suppose. First he asked us what assets we had, and that was a little bit embarrassing."

"Why was that so embarrassing? You have a respectable-sized estate, don't you?"

"Oh, yes, it wasn't that. But I've got quite a few assets that Harry didn't know about, and I felt I'd better come clean."

"How did Harry react?"

"Not too well. He demanded to know where I had gotten them."

"Well, where did you?"

"From a property settlement after my first marriage."

"Did that explanation satisfy Harry?"

"No, it actually upset him more."

"How come?"

"Harry didn't know I'd been married before."

"Uh-oh. How did Spindle handle that one?"

"Oh, he was terrific. He pointed out to Harry that it could have been a whole lot worse: my first husband could have been a pauper."

"Good point. Did that calm Harry down?"

"Eventually. But then it got worse."

"How so?"

"Don started asking us where we wanted to leave our property. Harry said he was going to leave it all to me, if I survived him, and he assumed that I would be doing the same. But Don reminded me that I could not do that since I'd agreed to leave half of my estate to my sister, Ruth."

"Why are you leaving half to Ruth? She's got plenty of money, doesn't she?"

"I made a deal with her."

"What kind of deal?"

"Well, when I married Harry I was afraid he wouldn't go through with it if he knew I'd been married before. Since Ruth was the one most likely to spill the beans, I had Don draft an agreement that if she didn't tell Harry

I'd been married before, I would leave her half of my estate."

"But now Harry knows you were married before, so why do you have to leave half your estate to Ruth?"

"Actually, I made the same point to Don, but he pointed out that since it wasn't Ruth's fault that Harry knew, I still had to leave the property to her. Harry was not pleased. He questioned whether it was appropriate for Don to have drafted this agreement with Ruth, when Don was representing him in drafting his will."

"How did Don react?"

"Rather badly, actually. He was extremely offended, since he felt his integrity had been impugned. He pulled a trophy out of his bookcase that depicted a bowler whose outstretched arm held the scales of justice, which Don explained had been awarded to him by his bowling league only nine years ago for honesty in scoring.

"He went on to recount how all twelve ethical complaints that had been lodged against him during his career had been dismissed by the bar association ethics committee, of which he was a past chair. And he offered to get letters from three former clients attesting to his honesty. Finally, he told of the time when, as a lad, he'd found a ten-dollar bill in the street and offered to split it with his friend, Nathan, not because he had to, but because it was the right thing to do. After about twenty minutes of this, Harry told Don to knock it off because he couldn't afford the legal fees he was going to have to pay to listen to tales of Don's integrity."

"And the rest of the meeting with Don, how did that go?"

"Oh, fine, I guess. We spent a lot of time worrying about things that are never going to happen."

"Like what?"

"Like who gets our property if both Harry and I outlive all of our children, and their children and their children's children unto the eighth generation."

"So what did you decide to do if that happens?"

"I told Don I didn't give a damn what happened then, that I'd leave all my property to him. But he said he couldn't do that because of some ethical rule, so instead Don set up an irrevocable trust leaving half of my assets to his grandchildren and the other half to the American Mortuary Association Charitable Foundation, which he says will give us a nice tax deduction."

"So that was it?"

"No, the worst part was talking about what Harry and I wanted to have happen if we got very sick. Don asked if we would like to have him prepare a living will indicating what we'd like to have happen if we become vegetables. I told him I'd love to."

"Sounds like fun. What did you cover?"

"He asked if we wanted to have food and water. Harry said he didn't."

"And what did you say?"

"No, no food or water, but that I'd like to have dinner tonight, if Don didn't mind."

"Was that the end of it?"

"No. Harry said that not only did he not want any life support if he became irreversibly ill, he wanted them to start a morphine drip to make it quicker."

"Did you decide to do the same?"

"Yes, but I specified that they try two Bufferin first."

"Bufferin?"

"Aspirin upsets my stomach."

"Oh."

"And then, finally, Don asked us whether we wanted to be buried or cremated."

"What did Harry say?"

"He told Don he wanted to be cremated and have his ashes spread on the pitcher's mound at Wrigley Field, but Don didn't think the Cubs would allow it."

"Why not? What harm would some ashes on the mound do?"

"None. But Harry specified that they be spread during the bottom of the seventh in a Cubs-Cardinal game."

"What about you? What did you say you wanted done with your body?"

"I told Don I didn't want to be either buried or cremated. I asked him if his form living will had a provision that would call for me to be stuffed, and have the girls trade off hanging me over their mantle—so they'd remember their dear old mom."

Surveying the Situation

STRUGGLING LIKE MOST FIRMS to maintain their preeminent position in the marketplace in this era of law firm competition, the Fairweather firm engaged their long-time consultants, Tellem, Whathey, Noh, to analyze and report upon their current financial position and the impact of their relations with clients on that financial position. Here is a portion of TWN's report to the firm.

Background

At your request, we analyzed the source of your revenues over the past three years. During that period, fee income attributable to clients the firm had served for five or more years increased from 62% of fee income to 71% of that income. During the same period, fee income attributable to clients who had not been clients of the firm for four or more years decreased from 40% to 35%. During a longer period, fee income attributable to clients who had been clients of the firm for more than two months, was 322% higher than fee income from clients whose names begin with the letters F through K. None of these numbers add up to 100%, but we rechecked them several times and can verify their accuracy.

At the same time, non-fee income as a percentage of fee income increased from 4% to 18% during the latest two-year period, attributable primarily to new charges instituted by the firm for photocopying ($.62 per page), faxing ($5.89 per page to receive and $4.74 to send, for it is better to receive than send), conference rooms ($25-$100 per hour, depending on size) and coffee ($1.12 per cup; $.40 for refills; $2.50 for capuccino). At first blush, this would seem to suggest that the firm should discontinue its legal business and concentrate on non-fee activities. At second blush, it suggests the same thing.

Because nobody could make too much sense out of this financial analysis, we thought a survey would be a terrific idea. So we designed two surveys—one for clients and one for potential clients. This report fills you in on the many interesting things we learned from the surveys.

Survey Results

Rather than attempt to summarize the results of the questionnaires, we thought it best to give you selected direct responses by clients to survey questions. This would both give you information straight from the horses' (clients') mouths and avoid our having to sift through a large volume of boring material. Set forth below, then, are the survey questions and selected answers:

Client Survey

1. How did you become a client of the Fairweather firm?
    My father was a friend of Stanley Fairweather.
    I met Stanley Fairweather at the Bigwig Club.
    I've always felt Uncle Stanley was a fine lawyer.
    Stanley Fairweather impressed me when he was representing the other side of a transaction.
    I was referred to Stanley Fairweather by my accountant.
    I was kidnapped by Nails Nuttree from the reception area of another law firm.
    I saw Stanley Fairweather interviewed on TV.
    Can't remember.

2. What are the greatest strengths of the Fairweather firm?
> Stanley Fairweather (4)
> The responsiveness of its lawyers.
> Nice views from their offices.
> Firm validates parking for garage in building.
> Convenient to shopping.

3. What are the greatest weaknesses of the Fairweather firm?
> Lack of responsiveness in lawyers.
> Lose too damn many lawsuits.
> Fees are too high.
> Stuffy as hell.
> Only one Stanley Fairweather.

4. What could the Fairweather firm do to better serve you?
> Win more often.
> Slice fees in half.
> Talk like regular people, not like lawyers.
> Make house calls.
> Return my phone calls.

5. Do you intend to continue to use the Fairweather firm?
> I suppose.
> As long as Stanley Fairweather's there.
> Sure, it would be too much trouble to switch.
> Of course, Uncle Stanley would kill me.
> Unless something better comes along.
> 'Til hell freezes over and all the little devils go ice skating.

Non-Client Survey

1. Why do you not currently use the Fairweather law firm?
> The who? Never heard of them. (5)
> Too expensive.
> One law firm is more than enough, thank you.
> We're not in deep enough trouble.

2. What would convince you to begin using the Fairweather firm?

> Death or disbarment of my present lawyer.
> A clear sign from a higher power.
> If you hired my son, Izzy, who is now practicing with the law firm I currently use.
> If they would represent me pro bono.
> A fortune cookie message that said, "Use Fairweather firm."

3. Would you be willing to meet with representatives of the Fairweather firm to discuss possible representation?

> Not on your life. (6)
> Sure, in their box at the United Center for a Bulls' playoff game.
> Yes, of course, but I'm afraid I'm tied up this year and next.
> Why would we?

Analysis

The firm's present financial position appears to be somewhat tenuous, and prospects for improvement do not look encouraging. Most of the firm's clients seem to have been attracted by Stanley Fairweather. While those clients appear to be extremely loyal to him, dependence on Stanley poses obvious problems, should he, for example, decide to die.

Many of the prospective new clients we surveyed appeared not to have any idea what the firm did. Several others had an idea, but the wrong one. Three of those surveyed thought the firm was an ad agency; two were quite certain it was a dry cleaner's. This could prove an impediment to attracting them to the firm for future legal business, though it does suggest several other prospective lines of business.

Recommendations

The results of the survey suggest several courses of action the firm may take in seeking to improve or assure its financial position.

1. Purchase a hefty insurance policy on the life of Stanley Fairweather.

2. Keep apace of emerging scientific developments that may produce ways of cloning Stanley.

3. Place greater emphasis in marketing the firm's policy of validating the parking tickets of clients.

4. Train Fairweather lawyers to be more responsive to clients, to talk like human beings, to be less stuffy and to win more often.

5. Cut fees drastically.

6. Hire Izzy.

7. Develop connections with fortune cookie manufacturers.

8. Purchase more boxes for Bulls' playoff games.

9. Conduct additional surveys in order to update and refine the valuable information gleaned from this survey.

Conclusion

These are difficult times for law firms. Once loyal clients no longer are (loyal). New clients are hard to come by. Only firms that develop a sound strategy and follow that strategy like their life depends upon it are likely to succeed.

We suggest that you base your strategy on a three-legged stool. One leg should be to retain existing clients. Leg two should be to expand the work you do for those existing clients. And the third and final leg should be to add new clients. Though your stool has three legs, you must reinforce them with the spokes of respect, responsiveness and reliability—we refer to them as the 3-R spokes—and then, before you sit down on your stool, don't forget to add the seat of quality, or you'll wind up on your ass.

What's Eating You, Anyway?

You run a business, you get all kinds of customers, especially in retail. And at the Mahzel Deli we got all kinds, that's for sure. I want to tell you about our lawyers. Not the ones who represent us, although, God knows, I could tell you a thing or two about them, too. What the hell, maybe I will. Why not?

Real practical people my lawyers. You may not believe this, but the first time I met with them we discussed the risks involved in my business and they came up with this brilliant idea. They would eliminate our risk from people getting sick from our food by having every customer sign an agreement waiving liability before they would be served. They said they'd make it real innocuous, so that nobody would think twice about signing it. Here's the draft they came up with:

WAIVER OF LIABILITY AGREEMENT

This waiver of liability agreement is entered into this _____ day of _____199_ by and between

_____ (hereinafter referred to as Potential Sick Person) and _____ (hereinafter referred to as Tortfeasor).

Whereas Potential Sick Person wishes to eat at Tortfeasor's restaurant, and

Whereas, Tortfeasor is willing to serve Potential Sick Person only on the terms and conditions stipulated herein,

NOW, THEREFORE, in consideration of the mutual covenants contained herein and other good and valuable consideration the nature of which, frankly, escapes us, the parties agree as follows:

1. Tortfeasor shall serve Potential Sick Person such food and drink from Tortfeasor's menu as Potential Sick Person may order for the prices stipulated thereon.

2. Potential Sick Person shall pay the menu amount for any food or drink so ordered, whether or not that food or drink shall be edible or drinkable.

3. Potential Sick Person hereby waives any and all liability whatsoever that Tortfeasor and any of its employees or agents or their successors or assigns (hereinafter once referred to as Tortfeasor Indemnified Party) have or may have arising, directly or indirectly, from Potential Sick Person's visit to Tortfeasor's restaurant, whether caused by poisonous or otherwise unwholesome food or drink or by spilling scalding soup on Potential Sick Person or by Potential Sick Person falling or otherwise injuring himself very badly or by somebody walking off with Potential Sick Person's brand new coat. Potential Sick Person agrees to hold Tortfeasor harmless from any and all losses, costs, damages and expenses arising from any of the foregoing.

IN WITNESS WHEREOF the parties have set their hands and seals hereto on the date first written above.

_____   _____
Potential Sick Person   Tortfeasor

Despite our lawyers' assurances that nobody would raise an eyebrow at the agreement, we decided not to use it.

Anyway, as I said, we've got plenty of lawyers for clients. I mean, any kind of business downtown is going to have lawyers, because the place is lousy with them. Now I should stop here, because I don't want to give you the wrong impression—I love lawyers. Well, maybe "love" is too strong, but I like them. They're fine, really. So don't get me wrong.

Our restaurant's in the same building with a bunch of law firms. The biggest is Fairweather, Winters & Sommers, and we do more business with them than with any other customer. In fact, we do so much business with them that I have a full-time person assigned to their account, Herschel. I assigned Herschel because he has the patience of Job, and to deal with the lawyers at the Fairweather firm, day in and day out, it helps to have Job's patience, maybe even a little more, actually.

Let me give you an example of what I mean. The other day, we get a call from Nails Nuttree, one of their big partners. Now Nails is to difficult what God is to powerful, if you know what I mean.

Anyway, Nails calls down and talks to Herschel. "Herschel," he says, "how long will it take to make me a corned beef sandwich?"

"Poof, you're a corned beef sandwich," says Herschel.

"Very funny," Nails says, "everybody's a comedian. How long will it take?"

"On rye?" Herschel asks.

"Does it make a difference whether it's on rye or whole wheat as to how long it's going to take?" Nails asks. "Rye."

"No," says Herschel, "I'm just trying to speed things up by finding out what you want. Mustard?"

"And *I'm* trying to find out the answer to my question, how long it's going to take to get my sandwich. Yes, of course, mustard, what else would you put on corned beef?"

"Some like mayonnaise. And if I tell you how long it's going to take, you're going to change your mind? You got to have lunch, right? You're not going to get a corned beef sandwich someplace else any faster than you are here. Cole slaw or potato salad?"

"Mayonnaise? What kind of an idiot orders mayonnaise? The reason I want to know how long it's going to take is because, if it takes too long, I'm going to go down to our vending machine and buy some of those damn, stale cheese crackers with peanut butter stuck in between. Cole slaw, and a pickle."

"Who orders mayonnaise, you want to know? Stanley Fairweather likes mayonnaise on his corned beef, and some lettuce and a slice of swiss cheese. Your sandwich is ready."

"What do you mean my sandwich is ready? I didn't order a sandwich, I just asked how long one would take."

"You don't want the sandwich, Nails, just say so. I'm sure somebody else would like it."

"Well, actually, I was thinking maybe of trying the corned beef with mayonnaise, and maybe a little lettuce and swiss cheese sounds good, if you don't mind, Herschel."

"But I thought mayonnaise was for idiots, Nails."

"You can't keep ordering the same thing all the time, Herschel. You've got to experiment, try something new once in a while."

"So you want to try it with mayonnaise?"

"Yes, how long would that take?"

Would this drive you crazy, or what? And that wasn't even the end of the story. Nails decided that, with mayonnaise, the sandwich would be better on a kaiser roll, instead of rye, and that potato salad might go better with mayonnaise than cole slaw. It was at this point that Nails asked Herschel how much the sandwich would cost.

"Five fifty-five," Herschel announced.

"Five fifty-five?" asked Nails in disbelief.

"You are going to negotiate with me on the price of a corned beef sandwich?" asked Herschel.

"Is there room for some give and take here?" asked Nails. "And how long will it take to get it up here?"

"You want it delivered? Then there's a dollar and a half delivery charge," said Herschel. "And don't forget the tax. It comes to $7.44, altogether."

"But I could save the delivery charge if I came down and picked it up, right?"

"Yes. And you could save the tax if you want us to mail it to you out of state."

"Very funny. Look, all I'm trying to do here is get some lunch at a fair price."

"And all I'm trying to do is satisfy you so that I can get off of the phone and serve the seventeen people who have formed this line since we started talking."

In the end, Nails bought both, because the one without the cheese and lettuce was only four eighty-seven, with tax, and there would only be one delivery charge for the two. That meant that the two of them would be $12.31, which would reduce Nails' cost per sandwich to $6.15 1/2.

Naturally not all the Fairweather lawyers order out. Some come down to the restaurant to eat, sometimes in rather large groups. And we've had our share of run-ins with them.

For example, like many restaurants we have a policy of adding on a tip automatically for parties of six or more. Several of our lawyer/customers have challenged this practice as an unconstitutional deprivation of property without due process of law. When we pointed out that the policy was spelled out clearly at the bottom of the menu, they

claimed that this type of contract of adhesion would never stand up in court. We decided to stick to our policy, but some Fairweather lawyer groups have avoided the automatic tip by announcing that although eight of them would be sitting together, they were actually two parties of four, rather than a party of eight.

But, like I said at the beginning, I like my lawyer clients. In fact, I've even named one of our deli sandwiches in their honor: the Lawyer's Special Combo. It's made of tongue, baloney and ham—and served on a kaiser roll, with lettuce and mayonnaise.

There's No Place Like . . .

MOST FOLKS HAVE NO IDEA how complicated the homeless business is. Maybe it seems strange to you to think of homelessness as a business. But it is. Hell, everything's a business, these days.

Now, don't get me wrong, I'm not recommending that you consider going into it yourself. For one thing, it's a heck of a tough business. And, for another, I don't need any more competition than I have already. The field is very crowded. As the economists would put it, the barriers to entry are low.

I first got into the business about a year and a half ago. You don't, technically speaking, have to go to graduate school to be homeless, but I did. In business. I went from B-school to investment banking. I traded futures, and made a bundle at it, at first. That was in the bull market. They say a person shouldn't confuse wisdom and a bull market, but I did. I lost my Midas touch about the same time the market went south. And from there it wasn't long before I lost everything—and wound up where I am today.

I'm not bitter. Hell, I had a good run on the way up. The way down was a bit abrupt, a little like bungee jumping without a cord. But I'm young, and I've got my health, so I'll bounce back up, one of these days. In the meantime, I'm learning a lot about life, a whole lot more than I ever did on the futures exchange.

But to get back to the business of homelessness. I'm not talking here about the things homeless people sell, like that publication *Street Wise*. No, anybody would recognize that as business. I'm talking about just getting along.

Most of us on the street depend on the sympathy of the public. You could say that we sell guilt reduction. In that business we have some serious competitors—organized religion, to name just one. But organized religion is a more mature industry than ours. Our more direct competitors are other homeless people. And, since we're in the retail guilt reduction business, marketing and location are everything.

We homeless have two principal approaches to marketing. The first is to present a sorry picture to passersby. Adherents of this approach dress shabbily, appear unshaven and sometimes use props, such as children or pets. The other approach seeks to create a there-but-for-the-grace-of-god-go-I feeling in the passerby. Those who use that approach will appear dressed respectably, well groomed and well spoken. I have always opted for the latter.

Just as a person selling pretzels or ice cream would want a prime location, so, too, does a person selling guilt reduction. I was fortunate to acquire the spot right outside of the large office building in which the Fairweather firm is located. My predecessor at that location was forced to vacate because he landed a job as a real estate broker.

Over the last year, I have gotten to know many of my clients by sight, and some of them by name. Those in the Fairweather firm are immediately recognizable by the intent, earnest look on their faces, and by the leather briefcases that they invariably tote.

As you might expect, I get some pretty strange comments from the people who enter my building. Quite often, they come from lawyers. For example, I had somebody who I approached by saying, "help the homeless," grill me about the definition of "homeless." She wanted to know whether somebody who rented an apartment would be considered "homeless." When I told her they would not, she asked whether a person whose parents lived in a home, but who did not choose to live with them and had no abode of his own, would be considered homeless. I answered "yes."

Then she asked me where I spent the night. I told her that often I slept in a homeless shelter. She asked whether that shelter might not be considered my "home," then, and that therefore I should not be considered "homeless," as I was representing myself to be. She thought that the Federal Trade Commission might be interested in the type of misleading advertising in which I was engaging. I gave her the finger.

Another Fairweather lawyer, Herb Gander, who is a member of the firm's real estate committee, informed me that I was in violation of the city's zoning ordinance by soliciting in front of the building. He said that, if I persisted in stationing myself where I did, he would report me to the city's legal department. Fortunately, I was able to ignore this threat because my friend Sheldon Horvitz came by at the time and, upon hearing Herb's threat, agreed to represent me on a pro bono basis in a challenge to the constitutionality of the city's non-solicitation ordinance.

And then, just the other day, one of the lawyers from the Fairweather tax department, Rex Gladhand, asked me if I was a 501(c)(3) organization, because he said he'd be more inclined to "help me out a bit" if his contribution were tax deductible. When I told him that I was not a 501(c)(3), Rex said that there were some lawyers in his tax department who might be able to assist me. I asked what that might entail, and Rex told me that probably it would mean forming a corporation with tax-exempt purposes and then applying to the Internal Revenue Service for an exemption.

When I inquired what the tax-exempt purpose of my corporation could be, Rex said, "Oh, I don't know, maybe something like: to improve the lot of those below the poverty level who do not have housing, by seeking to educate those people in order to equip them to find jobs: to study the causes and effects of homelessness on the homeless, their families and the public at large; to educate the public about the problems of the homeless; to provide food and housing for those in need of them; and to take all action necessary or incidental thereto in furtherance of the purposes for which this corporation is formed."

I said that those purposes sounded great to me, and asked whether the corporation could then just transfer any monies it collected directly to me. Rex said, no, that I would need a board of directors for the corporation, and that they would have to decide what the corporation's assets would be used for, but that they could not simply be used to support a single individual.

I told Rex that was a problem, since my purpose in establishing the corporation would be to generate funds for my support. Rex told me that even though the corporation couldn't just give me the money, I might be able to apply for a grant, for example, to study the effects of homelessness. If the board of directors were to decide my proposal was a worthwhile project, then they might determine to grant me a long-term fellowship for the purpose of my study. I asked whether Rex might be willing to sit on my board of directors. He said that he was flattered, but would have to clear the position through the firm's conflict of interest procedures, which could take anywhere from eight months to two years.

At that point, Rex said he'd enjoyed talking to me, but had to take off for a meeting. He gave me a dollar and asked for a receipt. I said I thought that, since I was not a 501(c)(3) organization, his contribution would not be deductible. Rex said that, though that was probably the case, it didn't mean he couldn't claim it.

Anyway, I may pursue the 501(c)(3) thing. In my business, I'm always looking for something that will give me a competitive advantage. For example, though many of my competitors have limited their flexibility by accepting only cash, I have offered my investors a variety of forms of contribution. I accept cash, subway tokens, bus transfers, tickets for sporting and cultural events and, with appropriate identification, personal checks and credit cards (for contributions of over $20). You may think it odd to provide for contributions that large, but I offer my regular customers a monthly contribution plan that allows them to make a single payment on the first business day of each month, and then not have to worry about my soliciting them for the rest of the month. Many of them regard that as a great convenience. And I'm happy to do it because, after all, I'm in a service business, just like lawyers.

The Devil Is In The Details

THE FOLLOWING CORRESPONDENCE between Fairweather litigator Seymour "Nails" Nuttree and his client Harry "Skip" Deason relates to the case of *Blonden Interiors* v. *Fashionplate Industries,* in which the Fairweather firm represented Fashionplate.

June 23, 1993

Dear Skip:

I'm enclosing our bill for our representation of you in *Blonden Interiors* v. *Fashionplate Industries*. As always, it was a pleasure to represent you. I am glad that everything turned out so well.

Fond regards to Betty.

Sincerely yours,

Statement
For legal services in connection with
Blonden Interiors v. *Fashionplate Industries*. $63,777
Expenses in this matter $25,086
Total $88,863

June 30, 1993

Dear Nails:

Thanks for your letter of June 23, enclosing your bill. I was somewhat surprised at the amount, but perhaps I will feel differently when I see some detail, which I would appreciate your providing.

Best to Louise.

Very truly yours,

* * *

July 10, 1993

Dear Skip:

I'm happy to give you the detail, as you requested. I would appreciate your attention to this bill, as it has been some time since our services were rendered.

Sincerely yours,

Statement

Legal services in connection with *Blonden Interiors* v. *Fashionplate Industries*, including answer to complaint, depositions, legal research, and memoranda, meetings with clients, telephone calls. 736 hours, $63,777

Expenses:
travel expenses $5,684
photocopy expenses $12,800
court reporter expenses $2,362
donuts and coffee $4,240
    Total expenses $25,086
    Total due $88,863

July 17, 1993

Dear Nails:

Thank you for your response, but I'm afraid I will need more information, including the number of hours spent by each lawyer and the billing rate of each person. I would like to pay your fees, but I need this information in order to process your bill.

Truly yours,

* * *

July 30, 1993

Dear Skip:

I'm happy to provide the additional detail you requested. Unfortunately, I cannot provide the hourly rates of our attorneys since it is against our firm policy to disclose that information. I'm sure that you will understand.

Sincerely yours,

> **Statement**
> Legal services in connection with *Blonden Interiors* v. *Fashionplate Industries*, including answer to complaint, depositions, legal research, and memoranda, meetings with clients, telephone calls.
> Nails Nuttree - 3 hours
> Harvey H. Holdem - 42 hours
> Samantha Priddy - 180 hours
> Hiram Miltoast - 37 hours
> Alice Twojust - 385 hours
> Heather Regale - 89 hours
>   736 hours, $63,777

Expenses:
travel expenses $5,684
photocopy expenses $12,800
court reporter expenses $2,362
donuts and coffee $4,240
   Total Expenses $25,086
   Total due $88,863

* * *

August 8, 1993

Dear Nails:

Thank you for the information provided in your recent letter. While I recognize the names of Nuttree, Holden, and Miltoast on your statement, who are Regale, Twojust, and Priddy?

I'm sorry that you are not able to provide the hourly billing information that I requested. Of course, I understand your reasons for not submitting this information. Unfortunately, our company now has adopted a policy against paying legal bills where hourly rate information is not provided. I trust that you understand the reasons for our policy.

Very truly yours,

* * *

August 18, 1993

Dear Skip:

In answer to your question, Heather Regale is an associate at our firm, Alice Twojust is one of our paralegals, and Samantha Priddy is head of our library staff.

I have taken up your request for hourly billing information with our Executive Committee. Though it is against our firm policy to disclose this information (for reasons that I know you understand), the Executive Committee has voted 4-3 to provide this information to you and I enclose it herewith, together with a breakdown of who did what work when.

I trust that you now have the information necessary for processing our bill and that you will pay it promptly.

Sincerely yours,

Statement
Legal services in connection with *Blonden Interiors* v. *Fashionplate Industries*, including answer to complaint, depositions, legal research, and memoranda, meetings with clients, telephone calls.
Nails Nuttree - 3 hours; $525 per hour
Harvey H. Holdem - 42 hours; $325 per hour
Samantha Priddy - 180 hours; $20.65 per hour
Hiram Miltoast - 37 hours; $300 per hour
Alice Twojust - 385 hours; $60 per hour
Heather Regale - 89 hours; $120 per hour
    736 hours, $63,777

Expenses:
travel expenses $5,684
photocopy expenses $12,800
court reporter expenses $2,362
donuts and coffee $4,240
    Total expenses $25,086
    Total due $88,863

September 8, 1993

Dear Nails:

I am much gratified that your Executive Committee voted, albeit by only 4-3, to provide us with the billing rate information I requested. We are now in a position to turn your bill over to our legal fee auditing firm of Ketchem, Cheeten Associates. They will want to discuss with you, and every lawyer, paralegal and librarian who billed time to our firm, exactly what work your people did and whether that work was necessary and was done as efficiently as possible. They will also scrutinize your expenses. After receipt of their report, I will be in a position to discuss your bill with you and what portion of that bill we might be willing to pay. On average, Ketchem, Cheeten Associates finds that law firm bills should be reduced by 31 percent. Should you be prepared to agree to a 31% reduction in your bill, we would be pleased to process your statement now.

Thank you for your cooperation.

* * *

Memorandum
To: Fairweather Executive Committee
From: Nails Nuttree

The attached letter dated September 8, 1993 from our client Fashionplate Industries is self-explanatory.

Since we were aware that our client retains Ketchem, Cheeten Associates and that, on average, this results in a 31% reduction in legal bills, we increased our bill by 35% over what we would normally have charged. The bill also represents a profit of $4,800 on photocopying and $2,000 on donuts and coffee. I therefore recommend that we accept the 31% reduction proposed by our client.

Habeas Corpus, For a Price

HERE IS ANOTHER CONVERSATION between Snooker Gallagher and law school dropout Four-Fingers Hentschler, taped in the federal penitentiary.

"What're you up to, Four-Fingers? Haven't seen ya in a while?" Snooker Gallagher asked his friend, Four-Fingers Hentschler.

"I've been researchin."

"What kinda researchin?"

"Legal researchin. Prisners got a right to go to the law library."

"Yaa, I know, but why would you want to waste your time in there?"

"Well, I'm not exactly pressed for time. I find that I can squeeze a couple hours a day into my busy schedule without upsetting it too much."

"Are you thinkin bout goin back to law school when you get out?"

"Nope, I told you, semester and a half's bout all the law school a fella needs."

"Then why're ya researchin?"

"I'm in bizness."

"What kinda bizness?"

"Law bizness."

"Yur not makin sense. Whatreya talkin about?"

"Even after you're convicted of a crime, ya got a whole bunch of rights that might spring ya."

"Such as?"

"Well, the major one is somethin they call habeas corpus."

"What the hell's that?"

"Some Latin phrase that means you should have the body. It gets you in front of a judge so he can figgur out whether you're bein held lawfully or not."

"What do ya mean held lawfully? Course yur held lawfully. They held a trial and found you guilty, for Petesake, didn't they?"

"Typical defeatist attitude, Snooker. You wouldn't make much of a lawyer, tell ya that. No lawyer worth his salt thinks he lost just because he lost."

"No?"

"Course not. There's post-trial motions, appeals, more appeals, rehearins, remands, retrials, hearins en banc. . ."

"So you get more than one bite at the apple?"

"More than one bite, hell; by the time yur through bitin, there ain't no apple left, maybe a bit of the core s'all, if yur lucky."

"And the prisner has these rights, too?"

"Course he does. *Specially* the prisner. Ain't nothin more important than a man's liberty, so the law does evrythin it can to make sure ta protect that liberty."

"And this habis corpis is fer that?"

"Exactly."

"And even if yur found guilty?"

"Course even if yur found guilty. If yur found innocent, you don't need no habeas corpus, do you?"

"No, I guess not."

"No, yur corpus is habeased out of there, already."

"But whatreya doin so much research for?"

"My clients."

"What clients?"

"A lot of our fellow prisoners have chosen to become ma esteemed clients."

"They have? How did they know bout yur services?"

"I've been marketin, that's how."

"What kinda marketin you been doin?"

"Handin out bizness cards, for one thing."

"Now whered you get bizness cards, tell me that."

"Made em up maself, down in the print shop. Wanna see?"

"Sure . . . Hey, these look real profeshnal, 'Four-Fingers Hentschler, 1/4 Attorney-at-law.' How did you get the 1/4?"

"Well, I told ya I went to law school for bout a semester and a half. I figgur that's a quarter what an attorney did."

"Sounds reasonable nuff t'me. What other marketin you been doin?"

"Word a mouth from my satisfied customers."

"You've got satisfied customers already?"

"Not exactly, but I asked people that retained me if they got any problem with me. When they say, 'heck no, Four-Fingers, we ain't got no problem with you,' I tell em, well then, pass it on to yur friends."

"So you've got not-disatisfied customers?"

"Yup. That's about the best most four-quarter lawyers do these days, I reckon. And I provide financin, too."

"What do you mean financin? Ain't nobody in here got no money to pay, so I figgured you must be doin yur work for free."

"Pro bono publico, are you kiddin? That'd be a laugh, wouldn't it: a convicted criminal workin pro bono publico. No, I watched my ex-lawyer, Harvey Holdem, and the only pro bono work he did was the kind that benefited his practice, so I adopted that same policy my own self."

"I still don't get the financin part."

"It's like you said, nobody in here's got anythin to pay. But, at the same time, I don't have no need for funds in here. So my deal is that there are no payments to make until after we're both sprung."

"Isn't that a little risky? What if they forget?"

"I thought about that, so I prepared me a little agreement that I have em sign. Here's one of them."

To wit, ipso facto, witnesseth and whereas the party of the first part, hereinafter referred to as "the Con," wants the party of the second part, hereinafter referred to as "Four-Fingers," to represent the Con in connection with his possible release from his current residential situation,

Now, therefore, the parties hereto agree as follows, to wit:

1. Four-Fingers shall do his very utmost to spring the Con, using strictly legal means and methodologies.

2. The Con acknowledges that there ain't no guarantee that Four-Fingers is going to be successful in springing the Con, since Four-Fingers is only 1/4 lawyer. On the other hand, the Con notes that the lawyer who represented him, who presumably was a 4/4 lawyer, didn't do so hot either, cause otherwise the Con would not be in need of Four-Fingers' services.

3. In consideration of a peppercorn and other good and valuable consideration the sufficiency of which is hearby acknowledged, the Con agrees to pay Four-Fingers an amount equal to what Four-Fingers thinks he oughta be paid at such time as the Con and Four-Fingers shall both be sprung.

4. This document contains the entire agreement of the parties and any amendment hereto shall be valid only if made in writing and signed by the party to be charged.

5. The titles of the paragraphs in this agreement are for convenience only and shall not be taken into account in interpreting the agreement.

6. The Con acknowledges that he has read the entire agreement, understands it and agrees to be bound by its terms.

7. In the event that any dispute shall arise under this agreement, it shall be resolved according to the laws of the State of Nebraska (which would hereinafter have been referred to as 'the Cornhusker state,' if it were used again, which it isn't going to be).

8. The singular shall include the plural and the plural shall include the singular, and never the twain shall meet.

9. Any notices necessary or desirable hereunder shall be in writing and, if intended for the Con, shall be sent to his cell, postage prepaid, return receipt requested, and likewise for Four-Fingers.

10. In the event any part of this agreement shall be found to be invalid, that portion shall be excised and the rest of the agreement shall remain in full force and effect, unless that produces a really stupid result, in which case, so what?

11. This agreement shall be binding on the parties hereto, their successors and assigns.

12. It's a far, far better thing we do than we have ever done; it's a far, far better world we go to than we have ever known.

In witness whereof the parties hereto have set their names and seals hereto on the day and year first written above or, if none be written above, then today.

——————————— ———————————
the Con   Four-Fingers

"Wow, Four-Fingers, that looks awfully impressive and official."

"Thanks."

"But one thing."

"Yes?"

"Most of it seems irrelevant."

"Course it does. That's what you learn in law school. Put down the guts of the agreement in a couple sentences and then dress the sucker up with lotsa stuff that don't mean much, but makes it look like you've done a hell of a lot of work, to justify your fee."

"But is that right?"

"Hey, we live in an impoifect society. You and I, of all people, certainly oughta understand that, Snooker."

A Risky Proposition

AMONG THOSE FORCED TO DEAL with lawyers against their will are investment bankers, who rely on attorneys to prepare prospectuses for their potential stock offerings. In the course of drafting these documents, the inevitable split between those wanting to sell the stock (the investment bankers) and those wanting to warn the investors of every conceivable risk of the investment (the lawyers) ensues. Frustrated by the results of a recent drafting session, investment banker Harry "Chip" Fitspatrick fired off the following letter to his attorney, Phillip D.W. Wilson III, at the firm of Fairweather, Winters & Sommers:

Dear Phillip:

    I have just received the draft prospectus that resulted from our fourteen-hour meeting the other day. As always, your prose was positively gripping. I found myself hanging on every word, wondering how (and whether) it would end. Indeed, I loved it almost as much as the prospectus you wrote for the 7% Convertible Preferred of Slasky Mining Company, which, if I recall correctly, the *New York Review of Books* proclaimed, "takes the genre to a new level, a must read."

    First off, I think we are going to have to massage the wording of the "Use of Proceeds" section a bit. Investors are going to be hesitant to plunk 14 million dollars into a company if all we can tell them is that their money will be used "to pay legal fees, and for this and that." Surely we can do better. You know, stick in something about retirement of debt, acquisition of equipment and the balance to working capital, like every other prospectus does.

Though I have comments on other parts of the prospectus, I have focused primarily on the "Risk Factors" section, and set forth my thoughts in some detail below:

1. While it is true that the computer business, which our client, Compustuff International, is involved in is highly competitive, I object to your statement that "everybody and his mother is trying to jump on the computer bandwagon." This makes it appear that our client is simply another undercapitalized, fly-by-night organization trying to take advantage of what happens to be the latest fashion.

2. While we're on that, I also object to your saying, "Although the officers of the Company have a lot of faith in what they are doing, Compustuff may be regarded by some investors as simply another undercapitalized, fly-by-night organization trying to take advantage of what happens to be the latest fashion."

3. As you know, the officers of the company are relatively young, averaging 32 years of age. I would have thought that that would prove a strong selling point for the company. You seem to cast the matter in quite another light, however, by saying, "While the officers of the Company are nice kids from good families, they lack the wisdom and maturity that officers of other companies in which you might invest would probably have."

4. I also think you are casting the business risk in an unnecessarily gloomy light. Though there's no guarantee the venture will be successful, I'm not sure you have to opt for quite as pessimistic a stance as, "There can be no assurance that after this offering the Company will be able to sell any of its products, or that, if they are so fortunate as to sell a few, that they'll be able to find a way to ship them, or that if they manage somehow to ship them, that

they will arrive undamaged, or that if they happen to arrive undamaged, that they will work, or that if they actually work, that they will not later break down completely."

5. The principal officers of the company are talented individuals who deserve to be compensated fairly. While some might quarrel with the level of compensation they will be receiving, it hardly seems fair to say, "The four highest paid officers of the Company will be making more money than their parents ever dreamed of making in their entire lives. And, when you add in the value of the stock options they will be receiving, many would consider their compensation to fall someplace between outrageous and ludicrous." Shouldn't you at least point out, in fairness, that the salaries are modest when compared with that of left-handed relief pitchers with 4.75 earned run averages?

6. Of course, the loss of key officers can adversely impact most any company, but I don't think we need to get into our officers' personal lives by saying, "The president of the Company owns a red Porsche convertible, which he drives like a maniac; the vice president for technological development's mother thinks she should bundle up more when she goes outside in very cold weather; and the chief financial officer eats like a pig, is grossly overweight and goes a bit heavy on the sauce."

7. I also think you overexaggerate the risk of law suits when you say, "In this litigious society, you can never tell what kind of claim somebody is going to dream up next. And with the way that juries are passing out punitive damage awards right and left, one unlucky case could very well wipe this fledgling company off the face of God's green earth."

8. Do we really have to warn investors about what they read in the papers every day? I'd delete, "This is a dangerous world we live in. There's war, terrorism, pesti-

lence, crime, depression, earthquakes, hurricanes, plane crashes, espionage, poverty, strikes, the flu bug and many other things to worry about. In fact, we would suggest that you think long and hard about whether you really want to invest in *anything* in this climate."

9. Though I guess it's theoretically possible that the computer will go out of fashion, I don't think that risk warrants our saying, "Though people think the computer is pretty important today, remember that they once thought the same thing about the steamboat. If they come up with something better than the computer—like, for example, a teeny-tiny little chip that they could insert painlessly into your brain, so that you'd hardly notice it—then this could turn out to be a really lousy investment."

10. Finally, couldn't you have let the individual risk factors stand for themselves, rather than conclude with, "While we have tried to think of everything we could that might possibly go wrong, we may have missed something. In fact, knowing us, we probably did. And that something that we missed (and therefore did not tell you about) could be worse than any of the horrible things we did tell you about, maybe much worse. So, in considering whether to put your hard-earned cash into this scam, don't forget the risk of the unknown."

Now I know that your job is to control the risk that we take in making this offering. But we *would* like to sell a few shares of this company, if for no other reason than to pay your legal fees. So what if we try to pare all of this stuff down, cut to the chase, as it were. Why not eliminate all of the risks you've enumerated and replace them with the following:

"Counsel for the Company and counsel for the underwriters have reviewed all of the risks involved in this transaction, and are both of the opinion that one would have to be out of one's mind to invest in this offering."

This approach would have several advantages. First, it would eliminate several pages of the prospectus and therefore save significantly on printing expenses. Second, it would be understandable. Third, it would make the offering a hot issue, since, given attorneys' well-known investment acumen, investors would probably flock to buy the stock.

I await your reply to this letter. My only solace is that, should you choose to ignore all of my comments, it probably won't make any difference—since nobody reads these prospectuses, anyway.

Respectfully yours,

Harry "Chip" Fitspatrick

Agent for Good

So THERE I WAS shootin' hoops, just messin', and I notice this guy standing 'round. Short guy. White guy.

I got nothin' against white guys; nothin' against short guys, either. I'm just describin' him, and he was short and he was white. I never had seen him before, not that I could remember, anyway.

This is in the gym. I'm talkin' about, at college. My freshman year. At De Paul. Blue Demons. Chicago.

Must be twenty, thirty minutes this guy's lookin' at me. Doesn't say nothin', just lookin' at me like I was some kind of racehorse or somethin', writin' down a few notes.

Finally, he says "nice shot," or somethin'. And I say thanks. And he says his name's Steve, and sticks his hand out. And I shake it, and say my name's Lajohn Elter. And he says he knows.

He asks me do I have a few minutes after I'm through, he'd like to talk to me, have a coke or a cup of coffee or something. And I say sure.

So that's 'bout how I met him, Steve. We went out for a coke afterwards, and I asked him how did he know my name. He says it's his business to know my name, and I ask him what his business is. And he tells me he's an agent.

Now I didn't have no idea what an agent was, and I guess he could tell that. I been recruited outa high school pretty good, 'cause I broke a couple state records, back in South Dakota. And even though that's not a place where you expect a lot of basketball players to come from, if you're big and you can score, the big schools find you. So

I had a lot of choices where to go to play college ball, but I chose De Paul 'cause, well, 'cause they just recruited the *hell* out of me, to be honest.

So Steve tells me he's a lawyer (though he doesn't look like one to me; no suit, no tie), and he helps athletes get themselves some money if they was good enough. And he thought I might be good enough, and maybe I might like to work with him sometime. And I said maybe I would.

I went back to my dorm, and I felt kinda funny. I couldn't think of nothin' but my mama tellin' me when I was maybe seven or eight that I shouldn't take nothin' from strangers.

So, I run into Steve maybe every week or two. And we'd say hello and talk a little and maybe have a coke or a burger. And he'd always ask me how was I doin' in school and stuff, and did I need help with my studies. I tell him no thank you 'cause the school they provide people to help us athletes out, 'cause it's pretty tough, especially comin' from a school in South Dakota that was not what you'd call academically advantaged.

My freshman year I did pretty good with my basketball. They put me right onto the varsity 'cause one of the senior forwards, he hurt his knee in a game before the season even started. And Steve, he come to every game, and afterwards he'd meet me and talk to me 'bout how I was doin'. We talk basketball, but we also talk a lot 'bout school—and life. Bein' pretty far from home, it was pretty nice havin' somebody like Steve to look after me a little, and just to talk to once in a while.

'round March or April of my freshman year, Steve invited me up to his law firm. I'd never been there before. Man, that was one *fancy* office, I'm tellin' you. 'bout the two-hundredth floor of some monster building downtown. Firm was called Fairweather, Somethin' and Somethin'.

When they told me I had to change elevators to get there, I nearly turned 'round and left.

But anyway, Steve, he asked me what was I goin' to do in the summer. And I said I didn't know, I thought I'd go back home. He asked me did I want to play some basketball that summer and get paid, too, and 'course I said yes I would like to do that.

So Steve, he took care of getting me a job that summer. And it worked out pretty good. I mean I was doin' what I wanted to be doin' anyway, helpin' little kids learn the game, and gettin' paid for it. Steve also gave me some books to read, I recall, 'bout law and lawyers.

Come 'round to my sophomore year pretty soon. And now folks are expectin' some things from me, 'cause I had a good first year and all. Me and Steve are still gettin' together from time to time, like before, but now he's startin' to talk more 'bout my future and what that's gonna be like. He's tellin' me that it's important to start plannin' now, before it's too late. I have no idea what he's talkin' 'bout, too late.

Sometime in my sophomore year I get some calls and visits from some other Steves. Their names aren't Steve, but they start talkin' to me 'bout the future, too. And they tell me 'bout the guys they say they've helped, playin' now in the NBA and pullin' down some major bucks. So it's startin' to feel a little like I was back in high school again and I'm bein' recruited. I'm feelin' like a pretty big man, pretty important. But it also makes me a little nervous. I mean, what do I know 'bout the future and a million dollars? I'm just a nineteen-year-old kid out of South Dakota.

By junior year you could say I was a star, leading my team in scoring, rebounding and blocked shots, near the top of the country in all of those, too. The team's doin' good, made it to the final four in the NCAAs. I was an All

American, MVP of the Blue Demons, and most everyone figured I wasn't gonna be 'round senior year.

By this time I'm hearin' from agents left and right, each one of 'em talkin' 'bout how he can get the best deal for me. Steve's still 'round and meetin' with me, but he's not pushy like the other guys, who are startin' to want me to sign on with them. And they're tellin' me it ain't gonna cost me nothin' to have them represent me, 'cause all they do is take a little bit of the money they're gonna get for me, so there won't be nothin' comin' out of my pocket.

Now I'm not no Phi Beta Kappa, but I'm not dumb, neither. And I know the money that's gonna go into their pocket is money that is otherwise gonna go into my pocket. So I start thinkin' 'bout do I really need these guys. I can read the paper just like the next fella and I can see how much money people gettin' paid, and all I got to do, maybe, is ask for that money, and wait.

I start to ask some of these other Steves 'bout why do I need them and all. And they start givin' me a big song and dance 'bout how they gonna get me a whole lot more money than I gonna be able to get myself, 'cause they know the ropes and all. And they start talkin' 'bout up-front money and the length of the contract and bonuses and salaries and taxes and guaranteed and not guaranteed and endorsements and insurance and salary caps and playoff money and incentives. In other words, they start talkin' 'bout a lot of fancy stuff I don't understand too well.

In the meantime, I'm still talkin' with Steve. And he's askin' 'bout my future still and he's not askin' me to sign nothin' to make him my agent. And he's askin' 'bout what about after basketball; people don't play basketball forever, he says. People need other things, like an education and a family. And he wants to know how am I doin' in school. And he's impressed when I tell him I'm doin' real good, 'cause I am. So he tells me he thinks I should stay in school and do my senior year and maybe even go on to law school after.

So I ask Steve what he's sayin'. All of those other agents, they're tellin' me I gotta go pro now, be crazy not to. And he's tellin' me not to and he's not askin' me to sign no paper or nothin'. How come he's doin' this? I ask him.

Steve told me that he'd made some money practicin' law; not a whole lot, but enough; he doesn't need much. And he'd always been a big sports fan; most every sport there was he followed. He told me how he watched some of the greatest players there was perform for years, thrill millions of folks and walk away without hardly a dime and no real future, 'cause they never had nothin' but their sport. And many were taken advantage of by agents who advised them badly, even stole their money. Steve said it tore him up inside to see those guys he'd thought of as heroes go into their later years with nothin'.

So Steve decided he was goin' to do somethin' 'bout it. He was goin' to find a couple players every year and try to help them out so they wouldn't wind up like some of the guys he seen. I'm lucky I happened to be one of those guys, 'cause I followed his advice and finished college, and played in the NBA, and made a bunch of money, and went to law school after. And Steve never took a red cent from me. Don't tell me there aren't no good lawyers you can admire.

I'm tryin' to do my small part, too, to carry on. I established a scholarship in Steve's name, for an athlete who promises to finish school. I just call it the Steve Scholarship. I don't use his last name 'cause I know Steve wouldn't want me to. He didn't do what he did for fame. He did it 'cause he wanted to help some people, that's all. Steve was the only pro bono sports agent I ever knew.

I say "was" for two reasons. Steve's gone now. And there's another person followin' in his footsteps—Lajohn Elter, though that isn't my real name. That don't matter.

Playing It By The Numbers

I COULD HAVE GONE to law school. I didn't, but I could have. I thought about it, but I didn't. Instead I became an accountant. A certified accountant. A certified public accountant.

Not that I have regrets. Well, maybe a few. I mean, we all have a few regrets, don't we? Sure we do. But I don't have any big ones. I mean, about becoming an accountant. It's an honorable profession, after all, certified public accountancy.

I deal with attorneys all the time in my work. We get along okay. Most of the time. But, what the heck, nobody gets along with anybody all of the time, do they? No they don't. So that's no big deal, that we don't get along all of the time.

If you want me to get more specific, talk about the problems we sometimes get into, okay, fine, I can do that. There are times I get the feeling that attorneys don't like accountants. I'm not sure why. But they're not friendly to me, I feel, sometimes. Well, "friendly" may not really be the word I am looking for. Actually, they seem to, well, look down on me.

Why? Well, I don't have the slightest idea why, and that's the truth. Sure I didn't go to law school. But, so what, a lot of people didn't go to law school. In fact, I calculate that well over 99% of all the people in this country didn't go to law school. So what are you going to do if you're an attorney? Look down on everyone who didn't go to law school? No, I don't think so either.

The fact is that I don't think they look down on everyone. Lawyers, I mean. I think they look down on accountants. They think that we're just pencil pushers. And that we're dull and unimaginative. Well, that is simply not so. First of all, for starters, *nobody* pushes a pencil anymore. We're all on computers or calculators.

Then, as to dull and unimaginative, well, I don't think that's fair at all. Sure, some accountants are dull and unimaginative, I'll grant you that. In fact, quite a lot of them are. Maybe most. But not *all* of them. Not by a long shot. To prove it, I made a list for you of what some of my accountant friends do in their spare time:

1. play paddle ball
2. work jigsaw puzzles
3. go to the movies
4. bowl
5. collect coins
6. garden
7. build model airplanes
8. play the accordion
9. read *Forbes*
10. bowl

And that's just *my* friends. I'll bet that you could find thousands of other accountants out there who do other equally fascinating things, too. So that should dispel the old, outmoded (but, unfortunately, rather widespread) notion that accountants are dull as cement.

And lawyers aren't so all-fired interesting, either. I know plenty of dull lawyers. Come to think of it, most are tax attorneys, with CPAs. But, still, they're attorneys.

Let's face it, though, our training is different than lawyers'. We accountants are taught to be precise. The debits have got to match up with the credits, the assets have got to equal the liabilities. And I'm talking about to the *penny*. We don't estimate or round off. No sirree. We are nothing if we are not precise. And we certainly aren't nothing, so I guess, if you'll permit me a little deductive logic, we must be precise.

Attorneys, on the other hand, are taught to waffle. The better attorney you are, the more you can waffle. Sometimes I think of giving attorneys I know a waffle iron, as sort of a gag gift. But I never do. First of all, they might not get it. They might think, "Why is that weird accountant giving me a waffle iron, for heaven's sake?" And then people would be talking about how weird accountants are and everything, which they do already, anyway.

Second, waffle irons are awfully darn expensive. And I work with so many attorneys that if I gave every one of them a waffle iron, it would run me a fortune, even if I could get a good deal if I bought a lot of waffle irons at once, which I probably could, though I haven't actually checked it out.

But I digress. I was saying about how attorneys are so slippery. You can't pin them down on anything. Let me give you an example. We certified public accountants are called upon to render opinions on financial statements of our clients. Those opinions are very risky, since, if we are wrong, we could get the dickens sued out of us. One of the things that can throw a financial statement way off is if there are some legal liabilities that we're not aware of. So, quite naturally, we accountants try to lay off some of our liabilities on our friends, the attorneys.

To do that, our international cartel of certified public accountants has composed a six-page form letter that asks lawyers for information about practically every aspect of their clients—law suits, potential law suits, contingent liabilities, non-contingent liabilities, what's the worst thing you can imagine happening to this company, now think of something much worse that can't possibly happen to the company and tell us about it anyway—and so forth. Boiled down to the essentials, our letter says, "Tell us everything." So we figure we've got those attorneys any way they decide to turn; they can't wiggle out.

But, like I said, they're slippery as all get-out. They've done us one better by having their international bar association come up with an eight-page form letter that responds to our request for information. About five of the pages in their form response are consumed by definitions of everything from "contingent liability" to "spaghetti," and the balance is spent limiting the scope of their letter. The upshot of their message to us is, "We're not telling."

The net effect of all of this is a letter from one side looking for ways to protect its rear end, and a reply by the other answering questions that weren't asked, in a way calculated to produce no useful information to anyone. Meanwhile, of course, the client is paying for all of this.

One thing about lawyers, though, is that they're experts at faking it, so you can't always tell just how slippery they are. I gotta hand it to them. Most of them have no understanding of numbers, or accounting. Heck, most of them don't even know whether the debits are the ones near the window and the credits near the door, or vice versa. They think that GAP is a store where their kids buy blue jeans, and that LIFO and FIFO are the names of their neighbor's pet bulldogs. Ask them to do their own taxes and they're hopeless, but get them into a meeting with a client and they can drop sections of the Internal Revenue Code like they were going out of style. I think that's what they teach them in law school—faking it.

Another thing they teach them in law school is question ducking. No, it's not question ducking, it's answer ducking and question throwing. Ever notice how, in a meeting, lawyers spend all of their time asking questions, and taking notes on those long yellow pads, which I guess you've got to be a lawyer to write on? Then, after the meeting, they dictate their notes into a memo, revise the memo, send copies to their partners and associates to read and comment on, then revise the memo again and send it out to the client with a cover letter, all of which gets billed to the client. We accountants, on the other hand, sit in the meeting, jot down a couple of numbers, go back and make a few quick computations and we're done. No wonder we don't make any money.

Like I said, I thought about law. But I figured that three years of law school would cost me about $87,650.86, by the time I added in all my living expenses. During that three years, I estimated that I could have earned $108,423 as an accountant. I calculated the interest rate I'd be paying on the money I borrowed to go to law school. I deducted taxes on the money I'd earn. I estimated the salary differential between law and accounting over the next ten years, assuming 3% inflation and increases in law and accounting salaries at the average percentage of those increases over the past decade. I figured that there was a 46% chance of making partner in an accounting firm, as opposed to 28% in a law firm. Factoring in all of these considerations, I calculated that, within eight and a quarter years I should be financially ahead going to law school, and that, thereafter, the differential would increase significantly.

Why did I become a CPA, then? Because I figured that anybody who would take the time and effort to make the calculations I did as to whether it was financially more advantageous to become an accountant or an attorney was a born accountant. So I decided not to fight it.

Lovely To Look At

WHILE PRESENTATIONS by law firms to clients have often been referred to as "beauty contests," the process established by Fairweather client Helotrope Mfg. Co. gives new meaning to that term. The transcript below constitutes the questions to, and answers from, finalists in the beauty contest Helotrope conducted to find a firm to represent it in a potential suit for breach of contract against Orton Incorporated.

Moderator: Hi. Herbert Lovella here, back with you all again for the exciting conclusion to our contest. First of all, congratulations to all of you outstanding contestants for having survived the bathing suit and talent show portions of this competition.

As you know, we go now to the last round, in which each contestant is asked a single question and has one minute in which to respond. These questions have been prepared by representatives from the Lawyer Person America Pageant and have been kept under both lock and key by our accounting firm, Greedy and Tite. Our judges will select a law firm to represent the company based upon your responses to these questions. So good luck to each of you, and may the best law firm win.

The order of your responses has been determined at random. Our first contestant is Ellen Jane Ritton from the firm of Fairweather, Winters & Sommers. Congratulations on making the final round, Ellen Jane.

Ellen Jane: Thanks very much, Herb. I'm thrilled and honored to have made it this far, and, frankly, a little bit surprised, too.

Moderator: Surprised? Why's that?

Ellen Jane: Well, this is a litigation matter in which Heletrope is seeking counsel, and I'm a trust and estates attorney.

Moderator: Well, why do you suppose the firm chose you to represent them then?

Ellen Jane: I guess maybe it's because the bathing suit competition shows off my great legs.

Moderator: Isn't that a bit sexist, Ellen Jane?

Ellen Jane: Hey, this is business, Herb. It's a dog-eat-dog world out there.

Moderator: I see. Well, here's your question. "You have been granted three wishes, which will be fulfilled. What are those wishes, and why?"

Ellen Jane: Gosh, Herb, that's a real toughie. Let me see . . . three wishes . . . that's so tough, I mean, I feel like Aladdin . . . and they could be anything . . . holy cow . . . so many things are running through my head, I mean, this is like a dream come true, almost like winning the lottery . . . even better than winning the lottery, because I guess that could be one of my three wishes, if I wanted, and I'd still have two left for things like world peace or homelessness . . . but I'd want to be realistic with my wishes, because even if they say three wishes—anything in the whole, wide world—there may still be limitations. . .

Moderator: You're just about out of time, Ellen Jane, five more seconds left.

Ellen Jane: I wish for ten more minutes to answer this question.

Moderator: I'm afraid we can't do that.

Ellen Jane: Why not? You said any three wishes. That's one; now I have two left.

Moderator: I'm sorry, but each contestant has only one minute to answer. It wouldn't be fair to give you ten extra minutes, would it?

Ellen Jane: Who knows what's fair or not fair, Herb? Maybe it wasn't fair to grant me the three wishes in the first place, since nobody else got three wishes. But you gave them to me, Herb, and now you're trying to welch.

Moderator: I'm very sorry you feel that way, Ellen Jane, but your time is up, and now we're going to have to go to our next contestant.

Ellen Jane: You haven't heard the last from me on this one, Herb. I may be only a trusts and estates lawyer, but I am still a lawyer. I'll sue you for every penny. . .

Moderator: Take her away, please. Good, now our next contestant is Andrew Reitstarr, from LA. How are you today, Mr. Reitstarr.

Andrew: Hey, Herbie baby, it's Andi, with an "i".

Moderator: Okay, Andi.

Andrew: Yeh, with an "i". I'm doin' just super, Herbie, tip-top of my game. And you, Herbie, how's it goin' with you?

Moderator: Great, Andi. Good to have you with us and. . .

Andrew: Super to be here, Herbie, super, a real thrill for me to be here on the show with you. I've always admired you, Herbie, since I was a little kid, really. Super.

Moderator: Well, thanks Andi. . .

Andrew: Hey, don't mention it. We're speakin' from the heart here, Herbie. And the heart don't need no thanks.

Moderator: Fine, Andi. Here's your question. . .

Andrew: One sec, Herbie, can I interrupt?

Moderator: I guess so, what is it?

Andrew: I was just wonderin', is this being taped?

Moderator: Actually, I think it is. Is that okay. I mean if you have any objection. . .

Andrew: Objections? Heck no. I was just wonderin' if maybe I could get a copy of the tape, if it wouldn't be too much trouble. I mean I would be happy to pay for it. Look, here's a couple hundred bucks, Herb. That should cover it, keep the change.

Moderator: Andi, I'm sure you don't mean this, but two hundred bucks, this could be taken as a bribe. And, anyway, I don't have any part in making the actual decision.

Andrew: You don't? Here, give me those hundreds, here's ten bucks. Bill me if it comes to more, would ya? Who does make the decisions in this thing?

Moderator: There are five judges out there in the audience.

Andrew: Oh, I see. Well, HELLO THERE JUDGES! I love ya.

Moderator: We've got to get on and ask you the question. Here it is: "You are selected as the winner of this contest. . ."

Andrew: I am, hey, great, it's over, I didn't expect it so quick.

Moderator: No, the question is just assuming that you win, for purposes of the question.

Andrew: Well, you should make that clear; I thought it was all over there for a second.

Moderator: Well, I'm sorry you were confused. Let me try again, "Assuming, arguendo, that you are selected as the winner of this contest, you will have many opportunities to make money, some of which may not be entirely ethical. What action will you take to make sure that you are not led astray?"

Andrew: Good question, Herbie. Let me say, right off, that ethics has always been important to me. Heck, ethics

is almost as important as making money, but not quite; that's how much I value ethics. So first thing I'd do is set up an ethics committee to try to screen me from all the sleaze balls who would be tryin' to lead me down the path to the devil and corruption. If that didn't work, then I'd do the next best thing to avoidin' graft.

Moderator: Which is?

Andrew: I'd spread it around. There's somethin' in it for you, too, Herbie, 'cause even if you don't make the selection, you're an important guy, in my book. And there's somethin' in it for each and every one of you judges, too, SO PICK ME. I love ya.

Moderator: Thanks, Andrew. And now here's our next contestant, F. Randolph Rawls III, of the firm Archer & Babbit in Raleigh, North Carolina. What do you go by, Mr. Rawls?

Randolph: My friends call me Three, Herb.

Moderator: Okay, Three, it's good to have you with us.

Randolph: Good to be here, Herb.

Moderator: Ready for your question?

Randolph: Fire away.

Moderator: If you have children, what value would you want to pass on to them, and why?

Randolph: I would say "forgiveness," Herb, because I have always said, "if you can't forgive, you can't live." I mean, you just know in life that people are going to do dumb things, and hurt you, and what are you going to do, just carry a grudge all your life, or sue everybody and his uncle? No, Herb, I say, "forgive and forget." Remember, too, that "forgive" contains the word "give," so that when you forgive you also *give*. And I think that's very important. And the word "forgive" also contains the word "for," so that when you forgive you are *for* something, not always being a naysayer. Forgive also has the word "or," which serves as a reminder to us that, in life, Herb, it's always one thing *or* another. So I would try to instill the value of forgiveness in my children, Herb, because, as I always say, "if you're always trying to get even, you'll never get ahead."

Moderator: That's beautiful, Three, and now our fourth contestant is Fred Hightower, from the firm of Jackson & Hightower in Houston, Texas. How are you feeling today, Fred?

Fred: Wale, Herb, tell ya the truth, ahm jest a wee bit nervous. See, ahve nevah been in one a these contests before and ahd shure like to win for mah firm, cause, well, frankly, Herb, we could use the bizness. Things haven't been what we'd call gushin' in the legal biz down ahr way lately, if ya know what ah mean.

Moderator: I sure do, Fred. Now here's your question: "You and your spouse of twenty years, Felicia, have been having some serious disagreements lately over both personal and philosophical issues. Your legal business has fallen off badly. And, to top it all off, you have reason to suspect that Felicia is having an affair with your best friend, Ernest. Under this severe pressure, you have begun to drink heavily and occasionally have gotten a bit physical with your spouse in the presence of your three children, Timmy (age 11), Sally Ann (9) and little Jimmy (4 1/2), who because of a birth defect says 'like' every other word. How would you handle this sensitive situation?"

Fred: Well, Herb, first ahd try to get some help for mah drinkin' problem, because ahve seen how terrible an effect that can have on a family. Fact is, ah have a teensy weensy bit of a drinkin' problem mahself. Nothin' serious, but ah do hit the bottle pretty hard, two, maybe three times a day, tops.

Next, ahd have a little bit of a talk with Felicia to see whether we couldn't get things back on track. Ahd try to be real honest about what was goin' on and the pressures we were both under. I think people have t'be open, honest and understanding in resolvin' their differences. Course ahd ask her flat-out if she was diddlin' with Ernie, and if she was, ahd divorce that slut so fast she wouldn't know what hit her. Probably ahd take the children and hide out somewheres. Might leave her little Jimmy, though, cause those durn kids that say "like" every other word drive me pretty-near nuts.

Moderator: Thank you very much, Fred. Our final contestant is Beatrice Eflent, from the New York law firm of Anderson & Save. How are you doing today, Beatrice?

Beatrice: Fine, Herb. I understand you have a question for me. I'd appreciate it if you could ask it quickly, because I have several other meetings that I need to attend today.

Moderator: Yes, of course, Beatrice, sorry to be delaying you. Here's your question, "If you win this contest, you will be doing a lot of traveling around the country. What will you hope to accomplish in your travels?"

Beatrice: Well, Herb, I would hope to be a role model for people of my race, sex, age and height. I know that there are a lot of people out there who haven't been blessed with the same amount of brains and talent that I have. But that doesn't make them bad people.

I think that bridges need to be built between the genius and the dolt, and I would hope to be, well, a builder of bridges. I don't, of course, mean in the literal sense of constructing spanning devices of metal or wood, or whatever the hell they build bridges out of. I leave that to lower-class types who don't have too much up here in the noggin, if you know what I mean, Herb. The types of bridges I'm talking about are metaphorical bridges between human beings, bridges built not with grime on one's hands and sweat on one's brow—because, frankly, that disgusts me—but bridges built with words and love and wisdom and empathy. If I could build that kind of bridge, bring some understanding into the lives of eight or nine not-very-smart, perfectly ordinary people, that would give me a real kick.

I've gotta run now, Herb. Be a sweetheart and call my secretary, Wanda, to let her know I've won, I mean, if I've won.

[EDITOR'S NOTE: Helotrope settled its contract dispute by splitting the difference with Orton, and so did not hire any of the finalists.]

Trading Places

To: Fairweather Clients Association Members
From: Rebecca Fissure
Re: Fee Bargaining Status and Strategy
CONFIDENTIAL

This memo will bring you up to date on where we're at, how we got there and where we go from here with respect to our fee negotiations with Fairweather, Winters & Sommers.

As many of you will recall, some members of the Fairweather Clients Association felt that, though the advice they had received about their back problems, the FCA wiener roasts and the exercise of drafting association by-laws and articles were all extremely worthwhile, they had hoped that something of more practical use might emerge from the association's efforts. Jack Rite suggested that one interest we all had in common was reducing legal fees and that, as a group of consumers of legal work, we might be in a position to exercise some leverage to negotiate fees downwards. So Jack, Ben-Ben and I were asked to serve on a subcommittee to talk to the Fairweather firm about adjusting their fees.

Your subcommittee met to discuss strategy. First, we talked about who we ought to try to meet with from the Fairweather firm. I suggested that we meet with the Fairweather Finance Committee, since negotiating fees was clearly a financial matter. Jack pointed out that the Finance Committee, being used to dealing with cost-cutting issues, would probably prove rather hard-nosed about our efforts, and so we would not meet with much success. That seemed to me a good point. Also, since anything significant that the Finance Committee might agree to would be subject to review by the Executive Committee, I thought it might be wise to go directly to that committee. Ben-Ben was concerned that, whichever committee we decided to approach, the matter be held in strictest confidence.

Jack noted that meeting with the Executive Committee would still not get us to the real decision-maker, since all that committee did was rubber stamp the decisions that Stanley Fairweather made. He suggested that we might want to go straight to the top and talk to Stanley. Ben-Ben thought that would be an excellent idea, particularly since it would involve only one person and therefore be easier to keep in confidence.

We next discussed how to approach the meeting. Ben-Ben suggested that we might open with a little small talk, perhaps discuss a movie we'd seen recently. If we were to do that, however, he would have to take some time and go out to one, since he hadn't seen a movie in ages. He asked whether Jack or I had any suggestions, admitting that he was partial to thrillers that involved sexy heroines who appeared stark naked at some point in the movie. I took exception to Ben-Ben's sexist preferences in movies. Jack pointed out that this discussion was wasting a lot of time and not getting us anywhere. Ben-Ben said that that was the purpose of small talk.

I suggested that we approach Stanley with a factual presentation. We could prepare some graphs showing the increase in billing rates and in total legal fees paid by FCA members over the past five years. Another graph could show the increase in legal fees as a percentage of total expenses for FCA members. A third graph might compare the rates of increase in the other graphs to the increase in the consumer price index and the variations in the rate of infant mortality over the same period of time.

Jack agreed that the graphs would be a good approach, but said that he thought we needed to have a concrete proposal for Stanley. I suggested that we ask for a 15% cut in hourly billing rates. Jack thought we should propose three tiers of cuts—a 10% cut in partners' billing rates, a 15% cut in associates' rates and a 20% cut in paralegal rates. When I asked Jack the rationale for his three-tiered approach, he said that it appeared to be more well thought out than a simple across-the-board cut and, besides, since lawyers love complicated formulas, it would have a better chance of flying. Finally, by cutting partners' rates less than others, we would be acknowledging the greater value they brought to the table, which he thought would be a wise negotiating strategy.

Ben-Ben said he'd opt for a totally different approach that would not involve cutting anyone's hourly billing rate. We asked how we could do that and still hope to achieve our objective of lowering legal fees. Ben-Ben pointed out that the total legal fees we paid were a function of two factors: the hourly billing rate and the number of hours billed. By proposing to lower the hourly rate, we would be appearing to take money directly out of partners' pockets. Instead, he suggested, we should propose to extend the length of an hour by 10%, to sixty-six minutes.

Ben-Ben argued that lawyers have an emotional attachment to their hourly rate, but they have no such attachment to the length of an hour. Since lawyers were used to billing in six-minute increments, adding one increment per hour would be no big deal. In fact, he pointed out, if we extended the hour by 20%, by adding two six-minute increments, we could agree to a 10% *increase* in the hourly billing rate. This would allow the negotiators on the firm's behalf to return to their partners and say that they'd negotiated an hourly rate increase. We adopted Ben-Ben's strategy.

Our next step was to set up a meeting with Stanley, which we did last month. He was extremely cordial, opening the conversation with a discussion of a movie, a spicy spy thriller he'd just seen that he highly recommended to us. Ben-Ben thanked Stanley and said that he'd tried to get Jack and me to suggest a movie to him as a part of the strategy for holding this meeting, but had failed. Stanley appeared somewhat puzzled by Ben-Ben's remarks, but having dealt with Ben-Ben before, let them pass.

Stanley asked us what the purpose of our coming in to see him was. I said that we'd been thinking about legal fees. Stanley said he had, too. I said that FCA members had been trying to come up with a way of containing legal fees. Stanley admitted that that had not been the problem he'd been contemplating.

At this point, I pulled out the graphs that I had produced, showing the trends in hourly rates, legal fees, etc. in comparison to the consumer price index, and to the countertrend in infant mortality. Stanley said that it was funny we should point out these trends, because he had been reviewing some trends himself in preparation for the next partnership meeting. He went into his closet and pulled out graphs showing the increase in firm expenses over the last five years and the resultant decrease in earnings per partner. He said that he had more graphs in the closet that he could pull out if we wished, but that he didn't want to make this a war of graphs. He wondered if we had a proposal to make.

I said that we did and reviewed for him the alternatives that we had considered, concluding with Ben-Ben's suggestion for lengthening the hour. Stanley congratulated

Ben-Ben on his creativity, but said that his plan would not work. We asked why not. Stanley explained that this proposal would have to be presented to the Finance Committee, and he was relatively certain that they would not understand Ben-Ben's suggestion. This did not necessarily mean it would not be approved, however. The rule of thumb in the Finance Committee was that if something was too complicated for them to understand, then it probably was a good idea, and so they generally approved it.

We asked whether that didn't mean that our proposal would be accepted. Stanley said yes, that didn't mean that our proposal would be accepted. The reason was that the matter would have to go from the Finance Committee to the Executive Committee for its approval. Once again, Stanley was certain that this body would not understand Ben-Ben's proposal. Unlike the Finance Committee, however, the Executive Committee presumed that anything they didn't understand was a rotten idea, and so it would be killed. The process of moving through the Finance and Executive Committees could be expected to consume approximately nine months.

But Stanley said that he thought there might be another approach. What we were objecting to was paying so much money for legal fees, right? We confirmed that he was right. Well then, he continued, if we could come up with a way of your getting the legal services you need without paying so much money, we'd solve your problem. We agreed it would.

Stanley said that it was money that was causing the problem, so we needed to get rid of it. We asked what he meant by that. Stanley noted that many of the firm's clients were in businesses that produce products or services that the firm or its partners need or could use. If we could just trade some of what you do for some of what we do, Stanley suggested, we might both come out ahead. And you wouldn't have to pay so much money for legal services.

This seemed like a great idea, in principle. Trouble is, when we began discussing the relative value of FCA members' products and services against the value of Fairweather legal services, we found that there was greater disagreement than there had been over the amount of legal fees. To try to resolve the matter, Stanley has created a Fairweather Barter Committee, with whom our subcommittee is to meet next week. Stay tuned.

Postscript

SO THAT'S HOW others see us.

Long-winded. Cheap. Pompous. Irrelevant. Inconsistent. Self-righteous. Dilatory. Verbose. Disingenuous. Self-serving. Nit-picking. Condescending.

Not altogether positive. But instructive.

Strikes me, though, as a tad one-sided. Shouldn't we lawyers have a crack at holding up the mirror to those who wrote about us, give them a chance to "see themsels as others see them?"

In fact, I've got an idea about how to fund that project. We'll call it, "A Sociological Study of the Attitudes of Members of the Legal Profession Towards Certain Persons Outside of the Legal Profession," and the American Bar Foundation will snap it up faster than you can say . . . well, faster than you can say, "A Sociological Study of the Attitudes of Members of the Legal Profession Towards Certain Persons Outside of the Legal Profession."

Watch for it in a bookstore near you. Soon.